THE
ART AND CRAFT
OF
COURSE DESIGN

THE
ART AND CRAFT
OF
COURSE DESIGN

Tony Earl

Kogan Page Ltd, London
Nichols Publishing Company,
New York

Copyright © Tony Earl 1987

First published in Great Britain in 1987 by Kogan Page Ltd
120 Pentonville Road, London N1 9JN and in the Netherlands,
entitled "Cursusontwikkeling kunst en vakwerk", by Versluys
Uitgeverij b.v., Randstad 21-25, Almere-Stad.

British Library Cataloguing in Publication Data

Earl, Tony
   The art and craft of course design.
   1. Curriculum planning
   I. Title
   375'.001   LB1570

   ISBN 1-85091-367-6

First published in the USA in 1987 by
Nichols Publishing Company, PO Box 96,
New York, NY 10024

Library of Congress Cataloging-in-Publication Data

Earl, Tony.
   Art and craft of course design.

   1. Instructional systems - - Design   I. Title.
   LB1028.35.E37   1987   371.3   87-7668

   ISBN 0-89397-279-7

Printed and bound in Great Britain by
Billing & Sons Ltd., Worcester

Contents

Foreword

One of the greatest gifts each of us has is our intuition. This book is about the combination of intuition, creativity and logical thinking in solving one of the trickiest problems in the development of successful courses and lessons: the problem of making an optimum choice of design for the instruction that is to be given. Our own exposures to instruction tell us that the quality of designs (didactical strategies) can and does vary greatly. There are few learning experiences that all or most of the learners involved would rate as effective, valued, liked and also efficient. There are many alternative strategies from which to choose.

A didactical design must be chosen at the point in time that Tyler (1949) could have had in mind when he wrote:

'. . . . As the teacher considers the desired objectives and reflects on the kind of experiences that can occur to him or that he has heard others are using, he begins to form in his mind a series of possibilities of things that might be done, activities that might be carried out, materials that might be used.'

Many interacting and sometimes unpredictable variables have to be taken into account if one's choice of a didactical design is to be an optimum one. This is so whether the design sought after is for a unit of courseware in a computer-based course in Russian, a video that has to demonstrate techniques for stopping anterior and posterior nosebleeds, instruction on avoiding conflict between police and public in ticketing situations, or a visit to a museum in an analysis exercise over the style of Vincent Van Gogh. The road to finding an optimum design for a learning experience is always a fascinating one, albeit sometimes a long one.

Chapter 1 introduces you to some basics. It draws attention to the difference between didactical design decision-making at the macro (policy) level, the meso (curriculum) level and the micro (course and lesson) level. It suggests a definition for the term 'design' and explains the activities that design decision-making at the micro level involves. It introduces you to a special language of design, defines the term 'learning experience' and suggests a criterion by which the designer of a course or lesson can tell whether she or he has had success. These basics are essential for what follows in Chapters 2 to 5.

A design is first *thought up* and exists as a concept in the privacy of the designer's mind. It is then *worked out* and given concrete form. Whenever possible the worked-out design must be tested (with the help of a representative group of learners) and any necessary revisions made before the course or lesson it steers is installed and operating in the learning curriculum.

In Chapter 2 attention focuses on the process of *thinking up a design*. It proposes four decision-making aids or *referents* that can be used to accelerate and optimize this process.

Chapter 3 explains how to give a plan, structure and strategy of instruction (a didactical design) its concrete form. It tells you how to *work out* a thought-up design.

Chapter 4 introduces you to eight critical faults that are often made in giving a thought-up design concrete form. These can be met during the developmental *testing and revision* of a worked-out design.

Chapter 5 draws attention to the role of the designer once a course or lesson is installed. It touches on the subject of *ad hoc* (on-the-spot) designing in response to unanticipated individual learner needs. It suggests four critical questions for use in an *end evaluation* of a design.

The Appendix summarizes the concepts and ideas that you will have been exposed to in the book. It also gives you some 'design thinking' to do, either as an individual reader or together with others who have also read the book.

Cases and questions are used from time to time in the text. These are to challenge your thinking as a reader and also to validate the ideas put forward about the use of intuition, creativity and logical thinking in designing courses and lessons. At the end of chapters 1 to 4 are a number of tips. These tips are drawn from practice and are relevant for design decision-making at the micro level. They have served me well over the years in my work as a course and lesson designer; I hope they will serve you too.

Tony Earl
Utrecht, January 1987

Acknowledgements

In putting together the ideas in this book, I have enjoyed the encouragement and support of the Department of Research and Development in Higher Education at the University of Utrecht in the Netherlands. In writing the book my special thanks must go to a colleague — Ans Ronduite. Without the special quality of her critique and suggestions for revisions, the book would never have been completed. Colleague Jan Nedermeijer insisted on an introduction to a Dutch Publisher (J W M Baron van Boetzelaer, Director, Uitgeversmaatschappij W.Versluys, Almere) and so gave the push which started the whole process.

My interest in the use of 'intuition, creativity and logical thinking' in course and lesson design decision-making was first kindled by my colleagues and teachers in Basic Systems Inc, New York, USA back in the early 1960s.

For Ineke, Caddi and Harriet

We learn only from those we love.
Goethe.

Chapter 1
Some Basics

Introduction

What does a designer of instruction do? What is a design? Where does the design process at the micro level begin and end? Is there a special language of design? What is a 'learning experience?' How does a designer know when she or he has success?

What does a designer of instruction do?

'Oh, what do you do?'
'I'm an instructional designer'.
'Oh ...'

I discovered quite a long time ago that the only way to explain to an old aunt, a young daughter or a New York taxi driver what an instructional designer does is to give examples. If I was asked today, 'What does a designer of instruction do?', I would give the following examples from practice. They are taken from different levels of design decision-making.

1. A medical faculty requires their third-year students to spend five half-days in a general practice and visiting a patient at home. You are a member of the faculty team who has the concrete task of thinking up and making operational a successful 'plan, structure and strategy of instruction' for this encounter with the realities of general practice. You are the team's *instructional designer* working at the project's micro (course and lesson) level of design.

2. A new school for laboratory analysts has decided to create a problem-based first-year programme. You are a member of the planning committee who will draw up a blueprint for this programme. You are an *instructional designer* working at the meso (curriculum) level of design.

3. You are head of a kindergarten. You are alert to the need of helping children at an early age to care for the environment

of the planet on which we live. You decide to introduce 'Green Peace' projects in every class in your school. You initiate an exchange of ideas with your teaching staff. You have taken the initiative as head of the school but also as an *instructional designer* at the macro (policy) level of design.

4. A US Government Agency is concerned about the loss of life and injury amongst personnel fighting forest fires. The training department involved assigns you the task of devising a self-instructional programmed text to teach ten standard orders relating to safety:
   1. Keep informed on fire weather conditions and forecasts.
   2. Know what your fire is doing all the time.
   3. Base all actions on current and expected behaviour of fire.
   4. Have escape routes for everyone and make them known.
   5. Post lookouts when there is possible danger.
   6. Be alert, keep calm, think clearly, act decisively.
   7. Maintain prompt communications with your men, your boss and adjoining forces.
   8. Give clear instructions and be sure that they are understood.
   9. Maintain control of your men at all times.
   10. Fight fire aggressively but provide for safety first.

   The trainee population is scattered all over the western states of America and Puerto Rico. It is very heterogeneous and includes professional fire fighters, forest rangers, volunteer fire fighters and student fire watchers. If your product is a success, you will have had success as an *instructional designer* at the micro (course and lesson) level.

We make plans based on policy at the macro level of design decision-making. We turn these plans into 'curriculum statements' at the meso level. We design the 'courses and lessons' called for by the curriculum statements at the micro level. At this level the instructional designer is confronted with the very specific question, 'What design can I use in this piece of instruction for these students so that they will learn what they need to learn in a meaningful way and in a way that each of them values?'.

What is design?

The formal definition of the term 'design' as it will be used in this book, and as it applies at the micro level, is: *The plan, structure and strategy of instruction used, conceived so as to produce learning experiences that lead to pre-specified learning goals.* (The word 'instruction' here is used in its most general sense.) It is a definition which came to me after reading Kerlinger's (1964) definition of the term 'research design': 'Research design is the plan, structure and strategy of investigation conceived so as to obtain answers to research and to control variances.'

Although it is sometimes necessary to do some *ad hoc* designing in both instruction and research (in response to some unanticipated needs and circumstances), a design is created in advance.

Like the design of a shoe, or a painting, or a chair, or a spaghetti fork, the design of a course, lesson or a piece of research is something abstract. We know it only by 'experiencing' it. It exists first as a concept in the mind of the designer and is

then given concrete form. Its quality will determine, to a major degree, the quality of your experiences with it. In the case of a course or lesson, the design generates and steers (sometimes explicitly and sometimes subtly) the student's learning experience. Just how it will be experienced will depend on how good it is!

Where does the 'design process' begin and end?

The activities involved in designing a course or lesson are illustrated in Fig. 1. By name, they will be quite familiar to those of you who know and have used the so-called 'systems approach' at the micro level. Activity 4 in the activity cycle (Fig. 1) is the one which interests us most in this book. This is the step at which the designer looks ahead, and sets up and

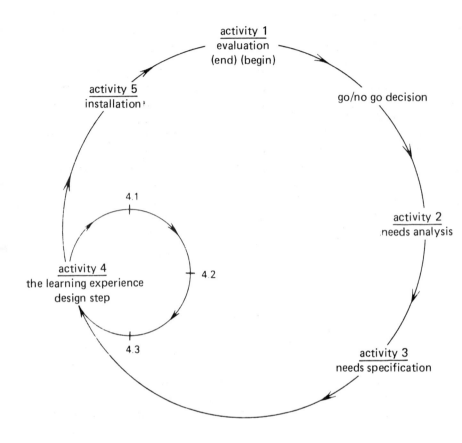

Figure 1 *The place of the learning experience design step in the design process at the micro (course and lesson) level.*

sequences the teaching-learning events that, as a course or lesson, will satisfy the needs identified and specified under activities 1, 2 and 3. Since it follows 'needs specification' (activity 3), and precedes the learning experience itself (activity 5), it is appropriate to label activity 4 the *learning experience design step*. This is the step at which all your creativity, intuition and logical thinking are challenged. It is close to the teaching-learning situation itself.

It is useful to distinguish three sub-activities (4.1, 4.2 and 4.3) at this step. These sub-activities (Fig. 1) have already been referred to in the Foreword to this book. They are:

☐ 4.1 Thinking up a design
☐ 4.2 Working out a thought-up design
☐ 4.3 Testing and revising a thought-up, worked out design

and are examined in detail in Chapters 2, 3 and 4.

An important premiss underlies the content of the activities named in Fig. 1. This is that a design *per se*, the 'plan, structure and strategy of instruction', is created *after* the needs have been analysed (activity 2) and specified (activity 3). The needs specification (activity 3) itself is in *no way* a specification of the actual plan, structure and strategy of instruction. What the activities named in Fig. 1 involve will be illustrated shortly with the help of a *case study*.

In this book the learning experience design step is seen to demand specialist know-how and didactical cunning. You have to be a bit of a scientist, a bit of a magician and a bit of a fox to think up, work out, and test and revise a design in an optimal way.

Is there a special language of design?

The answer to this, for design decision-making at the micro level, is 'yes'. The language you choose (out of the several possibilities) depends on who brought you up as a designer, and upon your own experience. I was brought up as a designer to value and use the *stimulus-response (S-R) paradigm* as the language of design decision-making at the learning experience design step. I still use and value it today. For some discussions, it can be a useful language at the curriculum and even policy levels. However, for most discussions (and for most people) the 'S-R language' is a singularly inappropriate language at the meso and macro levels of design decision-making. Its use can make people very angry.

The S-R paradigm sees any teaching-learning event in a course or lesson as a 'stimulus-response' event. The event (a lecture, a laboratory experiment, the analysis of a problem, a tutorial, a period of observation in a work situation, the flying of a kite, an educational visit to an art gallery, etc) must contain the appropriate stimuli (S) to which the learner responds (R) and, as a result of this response, learns. The S-R paradigm is the special language of design which this book recommends for use at the micro level of design. If the designer is willing to think in terms of stimuli (pictures, words, problem statements, film content, etc) and responses, and the association between them, the design task becomes a more concrete one. The S-R paradigm contains, essentially, the prescription for *any* learning experience. But be careful . . .

To use the S-R paradigm and its language does not mean, as Kendler (1961) has pointed out, that complex behaviour actually consists of S-R connections. As this same writer goes on to say, 'the concept of the S-R association, therefore, must be judged not in terms of its ability to provide a clear image of behaviour, but rather its *capacity to represent the facts of behaviour*'.

With the help of the S-R paradigm, the designer must use her or his intuition, creativity and logical thinking to set up an *environment of appropriate stimuli* to which the learner can respond, is willing to respond, likes to respond, and as a result of this response, learns. Failures to learn are frequently the result of inappropriate stimuli for wished-for responses or inappropriate responses to appropriate stimuli. The S-R paradigm and its language are, as this implies, valuable tools in diagnosing and correcting problems with course and lesson designs. 'Learning experience design' at the micro level is in fact to be equated with 'response environment design'. The designer's task at this level is to focus her or his attention on what produces learning: the stimuli (words, pictures, concepts, directives, etc), the responses evoked, and the associations between the two.

What is a 'learning experience'?

Tyler (1949) has provided a useful definition for designers working at the micro level:

> 'A learning experience refers to the interaction between the learner and the external conditions in the environment to which he can react. Learning takes place through the active behaviour of the student; it is what *he* does that he learns not what the teacher does.'

This definition has many implications for the design of instruction. We will come back to it again, directly or indirectly, more than once.

What tells a designer that she or he has had success?

Four words can be used in rating the quality of the learning experience generated by the design of a course or lesson. These words are: 'effective', 'valued', 'liked' and 'efficient'. They have been mentioned earlier, in the foreword. A learning experience is:

☐ *effective* when the learning goal is met
☐ *valued* when the learner found her or his learning time and activity worthwhile
☐ *liked* when the learning experience has been enjoyed and has motivated the learner for more
☐ *efficient* when the time and energy spent in learning what had to be learned is minimum.

To what degree a course or lesson is rated highly by the learners will depend upon the skill of the teacher (if one is involved), the quality of the materials and, not least, the quality of the design which generates the learning experience.

In this book, *Emax Vmax Lmax E'max* will be used as the shorthand form of 'maximally effective', 'maximally valued', 'maximally liked' and 'maximally efficient'.

Case study no. 1: The design of an educational encounter

Here is our first case study. It describes the designing of an educational visit to a doctor and to a patient at home. The substance of the story is from an article (Earl, Everwijn and de Melker, 1980) in *Medical Education*. It will introduce you step by step to the activities illustrated in Fig. 1. In this way you will have a better idea of where the learning experience design step fits into the whole picture of activities at the micro level of design decision-making.

Students in law, social science, engineering, hotel management, food processing, laboratory science and many other studies are often required to spend short periods 'in the field' observing the profession which they will eventually join at work. Such periods are potentially important learning encounters. They are a challenge to the learner, who must integrate what is seen in practice with the theory that has so far been learned. They are also a challenge to the professional, who must fulfil the role of tutor in the 'hurry scurry' of an everyday work situation, and to the learning experience designer, who must see that both student and professional like and value their time together. This case study illustrates how one such instructional design challenge was met.

In 1977 a project was set up to evaluate (*activity 1*, Fig. 1) and if necessary redesign an educational encounter for medical students in their third year of study at the University of Utrecht. The encounter involved a required visit by students to a practice and to a patient at home. The visit lasted five half-days. Up to study year 1977 only medical students who wished to be general practitioners (GPs) had to meet the requirement. In study year 1978 the requirement would be extended to *all* third-year students. Some 240 students would then have to make individual visits to a general practice and to a patient.

The staff of the Department of General Practice at the university were aware of some weaknesses in the existing encounter. An *evaluation* of the design of this existing encounter was begun. The group leaders involved wanted to be certain that the learning experience of the new generation of students would be effective, valued, liked and efficient.

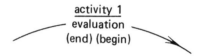

activity 1
evaluation
(end) (begin)

The critical problem was that students found the experiences in the field emotionally overwhelming. After two years of basic medical science they were suddenly confronted with the reality of practising medicine. The emotional problem was detracting from the students' basic liking for this 'encounter with reality' in the third year. It interfered with their ability to observe well. In discussion groups (before and after the visit to a practice and a patient), discussion tended to focus on popular issues such as what the GP's attitude to a patient should be.

The clinical reality of general practice got, as a result, too little attention. Some students tended to become too judgemental about what they saw, and this interfered with the learning side of the experience. A number of group leaders at the university, and GPs in the region fulfilling the role of 'guest doctor' to students, had limited experience of working with students. Many doctor/patient consultations were too short to serve as any sort of learning experience.

A 'Go' or 'No Go' decision to redesign the existing learning experience now had to be made. It took little time for the members of the design group to make a 'Go' decision. There was, for example, little or no opportunity to help group leaders and host GPs to perfect their skills as student tutors and so solve the problem via a *non-design* (No Go) decision. The solution to the problem was to *redesign* the existing learning experience of the third-year students. The time had come to go ahead and look more closely at the needs of students, group leaders and host GPs alike. It was time to move to activity 2 in the design activities cycle.

The *needs analysis* (activity 2, Fig. 1) revealed several things. If students, it was decided, were to observe critically and analyse effectively what they saw, they needed some frame of

reference, *into which* they could fit what they observed and *out of which* they could ask critical questions of the professionals with whom they would come in contact. This need for a frame of reference was seen as a critical one. There was also a need for more structure and clear intent in the discussions which the group leader had with her or his group, both before the visit to practice and patient and following these visits. Host GPs themselves needed to know what was expected of them. Inexperienced group leaders needed a 'group leader's guide' to help steer the group discussions and the exchange of experiences between students on return from the field. Some means of evaluating the quality of the individual student's observation was also needed.

As a design group we had work to do. It was the second week of March 1977. September — the month in which the new encounter had to be ready — seemed a relatively long way away. It was closer than we thought!

By the end of March 1977 we faced the task of creating a link between the analysis of the needs and the learning experience design step. This was the task of *specifying the needs* (activity 3, Fig. 1) in terms of five things:

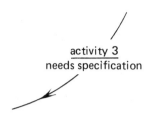

activity 3
needs specification

1. the specific end goal or learning objective
2. the evaluation criteria that would be used to signal satisfactory or non-satisfactory completion of the mini-course
3. the content through which this objective would be achieved
4. the method and media to be used
5. the constraints (the time, the number of host GPs available, etc) which had to be respected when making the design decision.

The *end goal* specified was that on completion of the programme the student would be able to give meaningful answers to seven critical questions:

1. Who is the 'general practitioner'?
2. What does she or he do?
3. What sort of decisions is a GP typically involved with, and how does she or he make them?
4. With whom does the GP need to co-operate?
5. Are all the activities typically 'medical' or not?
6. What factors influence the decision-making and activities?
7. To what purpose is the work of a GP directed?

The *evaluation criteria* for a successful encounter, it was decided, should be a report written by the student on her or his visit to the patient. The report had to cover the medical, psychological and social aspects of the patient's illness. These 'end reports' were very important in the eyes of the Department of General Practice. Together with satisfactory attendance at group meetings and a group end test, they were made the basis for the end grade that the student would be given.

The *content* was not formally specified. This was seen as unnecessary since it is implied in the seven questions and, with the help of an appropriate design, would have to emerge during group meetings and the visits to the practice and patient.

The *method* needed was the existing method: group meetings (guided by a tutor who was also a practising GP) plus individual observation. The *media* needed were a group leader's guide, student hand-outs (cases, examples, schemas, etc), transparencies for an overhead projector, the projector itself and a video for showing filmed consultations.

The *constraints* which had to be respected when a design decision would be made were: 240 students were expected in study year 1978 in the programme; only four half-days were available for group meetings before the visits, and the same number for exchange of experience and discussion after the visits; 12 group leaders and 100 host GPs were available; and the programme would have to operate with 20 groups of 12 students.

Past difficulties had been scrutinized. The needs were clear. The goals were clear. Constraints were known. Content was not explicit but clearly implied in the seven critical questions. The design group had reached the *learning experience design step* (activity 4, Fig. 1) in the activities cycle.

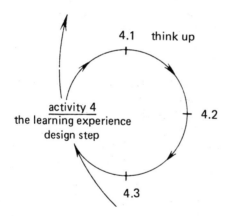

What design (plan, structure and strategy of instruction) would be best? Ideas chased and contradicted each other. Intuition, creativity and logical thinking set to work in *thinking up a design* (activity 4.1). There were several initial ideas; each member in the design decision-making team had her or his own ideas. The tension and excitement of thinking up a design had begun.

In the many discussions which followed, we were alerted to the importance of the frame of reference mentioned earlier: the *frame of reference* into which the student could fit what she or he sees and out of which she or he can ask critical questions.

Our thinking switched to the question of what this frame of reference might be. Several ideas were brought up, remained for a time in favour and were again rejected. Thoughts vibrated back and forth. Eventually an idea was hit upon which signalled a road to completion of our task of thinking up a design. This idea was to arm the student with a *concept of general practice* before going into the field. Initially there were different ideas about what this concept should be. Finally it was agreed that it should be a concept consisting of five elements, as illustrated in Fig. 2.

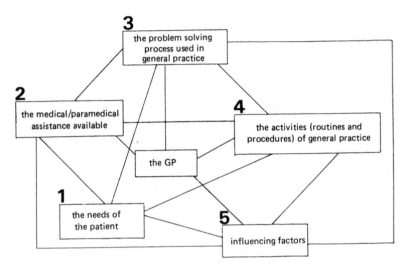

Figure 2 *A visualized concept of general practice*

The five elements in the concept are five things which have a critical influence in shaping an individual GP's care for the patient and in shaping the way in which a practice is run.

With the frame of reference in Fig. 2 in mind, we were able to see what plan, structure and strategy of instruction was needed to generate an 'effective', 'valued', 'liked' and 'efficient' encounter. We had our design. It was time to move on to activity 4.2 and give the idea for a design its concrete form. It was time to *work out the design*.

In the third week of April we worked with the concept of

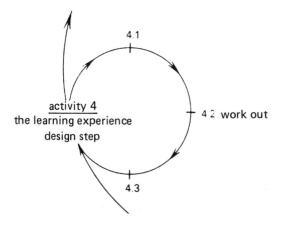

general practice and the specification of the student needs made during activity 3 and *worked out the thought-up design* (activity 4.2). The thought-up design required the *concept of general practice* to be established in the student's thinking *prior* to the excursion into the field. It could then be used as an 'anchoring idea' that could facilitate observation and promote meaningful discussion with the host GP. The concept, the thought-up design told us, should be taught with the help of cases on paper, consultations on film, group discussions, informative hand-outs and other stimuli.

Table 1 presents an overview of the thought-up worked-out design. It lists the topics, exercises and discussions that would occur prior to and following the visits to the practices. At the heart of the design and sequencing of the events in this educational encounter was the concept of general practice with its five elements: the needs of the patient, medical/paramedical assistance available, and so on. During the visit itself the concept was to be used to help the student see and discuss things in an effective way with the host GP.

The didactical design generated by the idea of the five-element concept was given its 'medical content' by three GPs in our design group. It was decided to compile a *Teacher's Guide* to help individual group leaders run sessions 1 to 10 and 11 to 16. The guide contained all the materials needed for the group sessions and also suggestions on how each session might be conducted. Host GPs (it was decided) should be introduced to the five-element concept and its intended use in a tutors' orientation meeting.

Table 1: *The programme showing S-R events and times involved*

Session no.	Topic/exercise	Time in min. (approx.)
1.	Introduction by group leader	30
2.	The needs of patients	60
3.	Medical/paramedical assistance	60
4.	The problem-solving process (1)	60
5.	The problem-solving process (2)	60
6.	The problem-solving process (3)	60
7.	The problem-solving process (4)	60
8.	The activities of general practice	60
9.	Influencing factors	60
10.	Final exercises in the use of the concept	240
Field *visits*	Students' visits to individual practices	(2 ½- days)
	Students' visits to individual patients	
11.	Exchange of experiences and impressions	210
12.	Discussion of a case met in practice	150
13.	Exchange of experiences of visits to the patients	180
14.	Discussions of reports	180
15.	Group answering of test questions	150
16.	Student critique of the programme	90

The following is a description of the teaching-learning activities which *one* of the sessions involved. This description will give you an idea of the sort of things which had to be scheduled, made and arranged when working out the design of the pre-visit sessions. In working out a thought-up design the designer's task is to prepare the 'scenario' for learning and assign teacher, materials and learners their various roles.

Influencing factors (session 9): time c. 60 min

Session 9 concentrates on element 5 in the concept: 'influencing factors'. These are factors which influence, or can influence, what a particular GP does and what decisions he makes. The exercises in this session are related closely to what has been covered in the preceding session. In session 8 the students have been introduced to and have discussed the various activities which characterize general practice and distinguish it from hospital practice.

Session 9 involves the analysis of the decision that a GP has made in *three separate incidents*. The incidents are described in a hand-out that each student receives. The student's task is to identify independently what, in her or his opinion, are the factors that influenced the decisions that were taken.

The first incident concerns a GP's non-referral of a 70-year-old woman to an orthopaedic surgeon for correction of 'hammer toes'.

The second incident concerns a GP's decision not to visit a patient in the early hours of the morning despite the angry message that the caller would get another GP to come.

The third event involves a GP's response to a patient with symptoms of rheumatoid arthritis and a depression which is disturbing her three young children. Accompanying the description in this last item are two quite independently given opinions by two GPs on what the GP in the case might best do next. The opinions differ. The students must identify what factors might account for such a difference of opinion.

To end session 9, the leader hands out the list of influencing factors, given in Table 2.

The group leader emphasizes that such a list is never complete but can be helpful to have when the student is visiting the practice and the patient at home. It can help identify what

Table 2: *Factors influencing the care given to a patient*

1.	The circumstances of the case
2.	The personality of the GP
3.	The existing knowledge and skill of the GP
4.	The GP's perception of what his role is
5.	Morbidity and mortality patterns in the practice
6.	The state of contact between the GP and patient
7.	The diagnostic/therapeutic philosophy and approach of the GP
8.	Point in time of the contact between GP and patient
9.	The presence or absence of needed assistance
10.	The past history of the patient and risk (if any)
11.	The size and location of the practice
12.	Others

factors are playing, or have played, a role in the host GP's decision-making.

By September 1977 we were ready. It was time to *test and revise* (activity 4.3) the thought-up worked-out design. We did this with the help of the third-year students entering the programme in September. We were wishing hard for a high rating against the *Emax Vmax Lmax E'max* criteria, and a minimum of revision work.

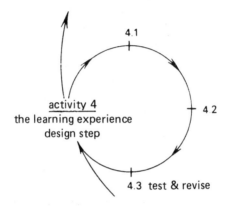

We scored high on some counts and lower on others. In principle, the learning experiences in the programme (pre-field trip meetings, visits to the practice and patient, and post-field trip meetings) were valued and liked by the learners. Points emerging from discussions with students about the use, or non-use, of the concept as a frame of reference for analysis and discussion of the things they met showed that thought was still needed about how to make the concept's use more effective and more efficient. The score for the whole learning experience looked, as a result, something like this:

$$\text{Effective } \pm \qquad \text{Liked } +$$
$$\text{Valued } + \qquad \text{Efficient } \mp$$

Students suggested that the concept was most useful *after* (rather than during) the consultation with patients, and *after* the visit to the patient at home. For the latter, many students felt that a second concept for viewing illness 'through the eyes of the patient' would be helpful. The concept they were using was mainly helpful in seeing the illness 'through the eyes of the GP' involved with the case.

The conclusions we drew from this try out of the design were that:

1. the conditions must be present in the observing situation for such a concept to function, and
2. the individual student must, in principle, value the concept's content and want to use it.

The redesigned learning experience was installed as a required encounter in the third-year curriculum with effect from September 1977. The most critical thing which had to be made clear to group leaders at the time of its *installation* (activity 5)

activity 5
installation'

was that each (when the time came) would face the challenge of teaching the concept in a way that was not too directive but at the same time directive enough to give the student confidence that she or he could use the concept as a *frame of reference* for observation and discussion.

The results of a first *end evaluation* (activity 1) told us that we should not be unhappy at the end result of our instructional design activities at the micro level of design decision-making!

A reminder

A course or lesson design process usually begins with the evaluation of the results of some existing course or lesson; this is activity 1 in the cycle of activities. It is followed by a 'Go' or 'No Go' decision. A 'Go' decision is made when it is clear that a problem exists which is a plan-structure-and-strategy-of-instruction problem. A 'No Go' decision is made when the problem and its solution are of another character. Activity 2 in the cycle involves identification of the 'instructional needs'. This is done with the help of talks with students, teachers, subject matter experts and, not least, by talking to yourself!

Once the needs have been identified, it is possible to specify them (activity 3) in terms of the course or lesson end goal, success criteria, content, method-and-media and constraints to be taken into account.

Activities 1, 2 and 3 bring the designer to the learning experience design step itself (activity 4). This activity has three sub-activities: thinking up a design (4.1), working out the thought-up design (4.2), and testing and revising (4.3) the worked-out, thought-up design. This design activity is followed by installation (activity 5). The cycle of activities is closed with an evaluation (a return to activity 1) of the thought-up-worked-out-tested-revised-and-installed design. The question is then asked, 'Must further adjustments or revisions be made before the course or lesson is run a second time?' A 'Go' or 'No Go' decision on this point is made. If the answer is 'yes', the 'Go' decision kicks off a *new cycle* of activities as changes and/or refinements are made. If the answer is 'no', the course or lesson gets its final stamp of approval. It begins its life in the curriculum as a standard, regularly offered course or lesson.

Some tips

1. A so-called 'SME', or Subject Matter Expert, for helping course design thinking, is not always the one who knows most.

2. Keep a 'crazy ideas list'. It will help you in many subtle ways.

3. Keep in mind what every sensitive teacher and designer intuitively keeps in mind: that each of us (Kübler-Ross, 1981) has four quadrants in our make-up; the physical, intellectual, emotional and spiritual. If we use the stimulus-response (S-R) paradigm without bearing this truth in mind, we will be using the paradigm in a *mechanistic* and *invalid* way. All four

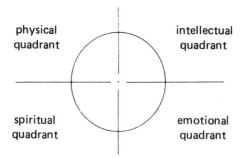

physical
quadrant

intellectual
quadrant

spiritual
quadrant

emotional
quadrant

quadrants in any design decision must be respected and cared for. We ignore them, as designers, at our peril!

4. If your design doesn't work, don't blame the student who is willing to learn. Blame yourself!

5. Write 'effective', 'valued', 'liked' and 'efficient' in your mind before you go to sleep tonight.

6. Do you like curious reflections? If so you might like this one from Spike Milligan (1973): 'A lot of learning can be a little thing'. It has a lot of relevance for the decision-making of course and lesson designers.

Chapter 2
Thinking Up a Design

Introduction

A glass jar stands on my desk. It is labelled 'Think Tank' and contains a piece of white cotton wool. From time to time it makes an excursion with me to a three-day workshop for teachers on the subject of design decision-making at *activity 4* of the course and lesson design process described in this book (see Fig. 1). This is the step at which the designer looks *back* at the needs specified during activity 3, and looks *ahead* to what should be happening when the course or lesson is installed (activity 5) and in action. It is a three-day workshop on the subject of the 'design of learning experiences'.

The glass jar and piece of cotton wool are used in the first day of the three-day workshop. This is the day on which we tackle the fascinating and challenging task of *thinking up* a design (activity 4.1).

The cotton wool represents the starting point of the thinking up process — a rather vague, emerging idea (or bundle of rather vague, emerging ideas) for a 'plan, structure and strategy of instruction' for the course or lesson in mind.

The jar represents the designer's own internal 'think tank' in which one idea after another will form, incubate, gain favour, lose favour, crystallize, regress, be tested, be thrown out, be worked on, put on the shelf for future reference, and so on until *one* idea is hit upon which is *it*.

Since everything to do with thinking up, working out and testing-and-revising a design begins in the designer's 'think tank', the three-day workshop has come to be known as the *Think Tank workshop*. Day two of the workshop handles the task of *working out* a thought-up design, and day three the task of *testing and revising* a thought-up, worked-out design.

Thinking up a design for a course or lesson is an intuitive, creative and logical process. Since it is a creative process it will not run smoothly from beginning to end. If follows the pattern Stein (1974) ascribes to any creative thinking process:

> 'The process does not run smoothly from start to finish. Work may be halted from boredom, fatigue, not knowing how to proceed, etc. Nevertheless, it continues or incubates on unconscious or non-conscious levels and from this work or from a test of this work there is a growing conscious awareness of a new possibility that illuminates and 'lights up' a new direction, another approach, a different pathway to the solution, which the individual did not see before.'

An experienced designer soon learns to 'sense' when she or he is on the right or wrong track. This is *intuition* at work. Richness of ideas, ingenuity in seeking a solution to the problem (the choice of an optimum design), and originality come from the designer's *creativity*. The disciplined weighing, testing and selection or rejection of ideas is based on goal-directed *logical thinking*. Intuition, creativity, and logical thinking are at work in a designer's think tank.

Although the born teacher, designer or teacher-designer comes up intuitively, creatively and logically with effective designs for class lessons, laboratory exercises, projects, group sessions, periods of observation in practice, and so on, most of us are not so naturally gifted. We need something to help us think up an optimum design.

What might this 'something' be?

The help which is offered to teachers and designers in the Think Tank workshop involves the use of four decision-making aids. The aids, or referents as I would prefer to call them (because of how they function), are shown in Fig. 3. The two-way arrows in the diagram tell you that the process of thinking up the design

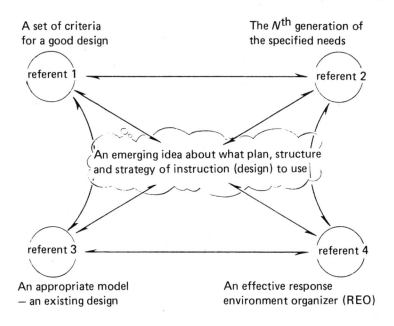

Figure 3 *Four referents that help you think up a design.*

for a piece of instruction with the help of these four referents is a dynamic one. The four referents and an emerging idea for a design interact constantly amongst themselves in the mind of the designer until a solution to the problem — an appropriate design — is found. Although numbered 1, 2, 3 and 4, this in no way implies a sequence for use of the referents. The mind of the designer darts back and forth within the content of each referent, between referents and in and out of the 'current' idea for a design. The process of thinking up a design is a heuristic one; it is in no way prescriptive.

What are these four referents, with their vaguely esoteric names?

Referent 1: A set of criteria for a good design

If a designer is to come up with an optimum solution to the problem of thinking up a design, the existence of a set of criteria against which to test an idea that is being considered can be very helpful. When drawn into the think tank, such criteria become referent 1: a set of criteria for a good design. Those

which I would use as such are the eight criteria listed in Table 3. Other writers on the subject of course and lesson design might well choose others, or add to the eight I have given. The selections I have made are based on their value to me in many different design decision-making operations. As a referent, it is very important that these criteria work for you and not you for them. When you work for them they are no more than a static list of criteria against which to check off the quality of the decisions you are making. When *they* work for *you*, they not only provide principles against which to check your decisions; they also, as a referent, are there explicitly to stimulate your thinking and give you new ideas for a design.

Table 3: *A set of criteria for a good design*

___

☐ Criterion 1: The design generates an active (not passive) learning experience

☐ Criterion 2: The design utilizes didactically meaningful responses and excludes non-meaningful responses

☐ Criterion 3: The design exercises the appropriate degree of control over the learning process

☐ Criterion 4: The design respects but outwits constraints

☐ Criterion 5: The design provides the learner with feedback

☐ Criterion 6: The design makes critical use of media

☐ Criterion 7: The design can be extended (as needed) with relative ease

☐ Criterion 8: The design is based on a systematic specification of the needs

___

☐ Criterion 1, regarding active as opposed to passive learning, emphasizes the importance of involving the learner — mentally and/or physically — in the learning process. An earlier quotation from Tyler (1949) drew attention to the importance of learner activity and participation: 'A student learns from what he does and not from what the teacher does.'

☐ Criterion 2 emphasizes how critical it is that a design utilizes didactically meaningful responses. Responses are the things which the design gets the learner to do via the stimuli (pictures, statements, materials, problems to solve, etc) which are brought into the learning environment. For a response to be 'meaningful' in the sense intended in this book, it must pass a certain test (Earl, 1973): (a) the response must be *relevant* for the learning goal, (b) the response must be *necessary* for reaching the learning goal, (c) the response must be *possible* for the learner to make, and (d) the response must be *effective*. An 'effective' response in this context is one which results in some increment (large or small) in learning, *or* some strengthening of learning that has already taken place. The response in question must be meaningful, whether it is a mental response in the privacy of the learner's mind or an open response; and whether it is specifically invited or is a spontaneous (ie not specifically invited) response generated by the design. Many courses and lessons fail because their designs generate non-meaningful responses.

☐ Criterion 3 alerts the designer to the fact that the 'plan, structure and strategy' of instruction chosen will assign control over the learning process to the learner, or to the instructor, or let them share it (see Fig. 4). To what degree the teacher and/or the student should have control at a given moment in a course or lesson is always a tricky question. Whichever way things go, 'control' or 'freedom' must never be aversive. Criterion 3 makes sure one doesn't avoid the tricky question. The best designs will always vary the degree of control given to or shared by teacher and learner — to left or right, for example, of the centre of the scale (Tennyson and Breuer, 1984) given in Fig. 4. Criterion 3 is very influential in the choice of a design.

1	2	3	4	5
Complete teacher control	Some student control	Joint control	Some teacher control	Complete student control

Figure 4 *Degrees of control by teacher and student of a learning process.*

☐ Criterion 4 requires the designer to 'respect but outwit constraints'. The word 'constraints' refers to the givens in the system — things which have been specified as such in the 'needs specification', and which in principle cannot be changed. What the designer must do is use his craft and ingenuity in outwitting

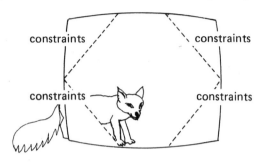

them. Constraints in the system include development schedules, money available for production, materials available, expert help available, and learning time. Satisfying criterion 4 calls for didactical cunning. You need to be a didactical fox.

☐ Criterion 5 requires the design to provide 'feedback' to the learner. Feedback is information on how you are progressing. It could be the correct solution to a problem which the learner has been asked to solve, the correct version of something she or he has been asked to draw or the correct composition of a cough mixture that she or he has been asked to make up. It's always nice to have knowledge of the results of your efforts in a learning situation — especially when you are getting correct results! Feedback is as important to university graduates in advanced degree programmes as it is to small children in kindergarten. Positive results and the knowledge that we as learners have of them, are highly motivating.

☐ Criterion 6, about the 'critical use of media' is telling you (as a designer) that the design you think up and use must not make *unnecessary or inappropriate use of media*. 'Media' here mean the hardware and audio-visual aids that can be given a role in a course or lesson. If you have ever sat in a lecture in which the lecturer projected slide after slide of information when two would have been more than enough, you will know what criterion 6 is all about. The critical use of media is easy to check. If the learning result would be the same *without* the use of the media (whatever it may be — computer, video player, set of slides), then its use is 'non-critical'.

☐ Criterion 7, about ease of extension, points a finger at a simple truth: a design can never satisfy *every* learner's personal needs. It tells you that it will always be an advantage to think up a design that can easily accommodate *adjunct* instruction for learners (fast or slow) if such proves to be necessary.

☐ Criterion 8, about a design having to be based on a systematic specification of the learning needs, honours the discipline of the 'systems approach' in course and lesson design decision-making. At the same time it implicitly reaffirms the fundamental premiss that 'thinking up, working out and testing-and-revising a design for a course or lesson' is something in its own right. It occurs *after* the needs have been specified. If the design you have thought up is not based on a specification of the needs, then the chances are that the course or lesson you are making will be based on *your needs* as a learner and not on the needs of the real learner population. You could well find that you are making the course or lesson for yourself!

Here is a way to enable you to 'feel' how the eight criteria for a good design can function as referent 1 in a designer's think tank. Think about a subject that you like, know well and could teach. It doesn't matter what it is — reading a finger print, making jam, setting up a distillation apparatus, laying a table, fishing, or the Battle of Hastings. Think about what the subject is going to cover. Think about how you would teach it.

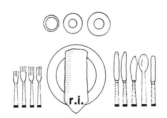

Think about your plan, structure and strategy of instruction. Now let your mind rove back and forth, over and amongst the eight criteria for a good design. Turn back to Table 3 (page 34) if you need to. Try to 'feel' the influence of these eight criteria on your idea for a design.

What are the criteria saying to your intuition? To your creativity? Do they make you think more logically and carefully?

Are they changing your first idea for a plan, structure and strategy of instruction? Are they telling you to throw this first idea out? to keep it at all costs? If they do all or some of these things, then these criteria for a good design are working for *you*, not you for *them*. That's how it should be. The criteria are working for *you*, in *your* think tank, as *your* referent 1.

Referent 2: The nth generation of the specified needs

Think about designing a course for teaching six-year-olds to tell the time. Let digital watches, cuckoo clocks and every other sort of clock chase each other through your mind . . . . Have you ever had to teach a child to tell the time? If so, what were the difficulties? What strategies would you think of using?

How would you test that the six-year-olds (by the end of the course) had learned what you wanted them to learn? Would you be content with having them demonstrate that they can 'say' what various times are on a clock they are shown, or would you want them also to tell you how many minutes there are in an hour and how many seconds there are in a minute, and so on?

In thinking about these things you are touching on the content of referent 2: the nth generation of the specified needs. The content of referent 2 is the design decision-maker's *current* specification of what end goal needs to be met; what criteria can be used to test achievement of this goal; what concepts, principles, information, etc (ie course content) will be covered in reaching the goal; what method-and-media is needed; and what constraints must be taken into account. The word 'current' in this context is very important. The content of referent 2 changes subtly from moment to moment as the designer thinks up her or his plan, structure and strategy of instruction. Referent 2 is a sort of 'databank' which is constantly being corrected and updated as the ideas for a design ebb and flow and vibrate in the designer's mind. In the Think Tank workshop, referent 2 is represented as in Fig. 5.

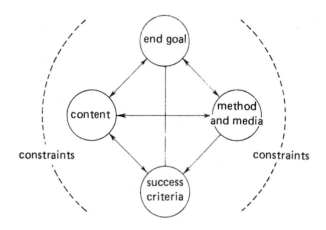

Figure 5 *The Content of Referent 2.*

The first generation of data in referent 2 is the specification made in activity 3 in the cycle of course making activities (see Fig. 1). The succeeding generations (of which there can be many) are the result of the intuitive, creative and logical thinking of the designer as she or he thinks up a plan, structure and strategy of instruction (activity 4.1). The content of referent 2 at any moment in time can conveniently be labelled the nth generation of data in this databank. The arrows in Fig. 5 are there to remind you that the end goal, success criteria, content and method-and-media must always complement each other. The dashed outer lines are there to tell you that you have to make your design decisions within the limits imposed by identified constraints.

As with referent 1, it is important to make referent 2 work for you when thinking up a design. Go in and out of the referent as *you* need to. Make use of one or more or all of the five elements as *you* need to. Referent 2 contains the basic ingredient for *your* design decision-making. If you have to, go away from referent 2 for a time and think *without* it. Creativity needs lots of freedom. You'll come back to referent 2 again in your own good time; when, for example, you need to check the logic of your creative thinking, or when you need to validate your intuitive thinking. Referent 2 is always ready to serve your decision-making. It is a tool for monitoring your logical thinking about a plan, structure and strategy of instruction.

Referent 3: An appropriate model (an existing design)

Thinking up a design takes time: before the optimum design is found a lot of mental effort will be demanded.

It can be nice to have something to accelerate the process. This is what referent 3: an appropriate model is for. By using an 'appropriate model' the designer is making use of an existing

solution (an existing design) to a problem. Having such a referent can be very time-saving. The other three referents ensure that the existing design is indeed an appropriate one. Their presence gives some guarantee that only those features in the model which have relevance for the designer's own instruction are transplanted into the design she or he chooses. They also discourage direct transplantation of a design. Direct transplantations seldom work. More important, the practice also kills originality; and originality in a design is a quality that students invariably welcome.

Every time you meet a design that you like, write notes about it, 'diagram it' and put it in your archive. One day you will find it useful as your referent 3. Below is a description of a model that many teachers in the Think Tank workshop have liked. It may well be found in their archives under the name 'fishbone': this is the name I gave it in the workshop. The basic plan, structure and strategy of instruction which it contains has been used in many different settings — encounters with the scientific method of enquiry for first-year Botany students at the University of Utrecht, encounters with the 'joys and sorrows in life' in projects in eschatology and reflection for young priests in training in a seminary in Yogyakarta in Indonesia, and most recently in designing a course for waiters in the dining room of The Fox Hotel in a rural part of England. The model could also serve as a model to help design the course on teaching six-year-olds to tell the time.

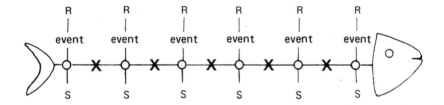

Figure 6 *The fishbone model.*

The fishbone model (Fig. 6) is essentially very simple. Each vertebra represents a distinct teaching-learning event. The 'S' under each event is the input (stimulus) in the form of information, materials, criteria for decision-making, etc, which is needed for that event. The 'R' above each event is the response that the materials, information, etc, must evoke. This 'R' could be a solution to a problem, a write-up of an observation made in practice, a diagnosis, a correctly laid table or a correctly cooked egg. The small stars along the backbone in the model indicate interventions by a teacher or guide. During these interventions the learner has the opportunity to get feedback on her or his performance in the S-R event just completed, to ask questions, to get more information, or to learn what the following event involves. The designer may choose to start with the event nearest the tail or with the event at the head and work backwards. (This latter model of sequence is known as 'backward chaining'; you'll meet an example of it later in this book.)

Figure 7 illustrates the fishbone model as it was used in training waiters at The Fox Hotel. Five discrete events were identified which were concerned with receiving, serving and taking leave of the hotel guests. These events are named along the vertebrae of the fish in chronological order. For each event a teaching-learning situation was made. The information and other stimuli (S) needed for training in each situation were chosen. The things (R) which the trainee would have to demonstrate that she or he could do during and at the end of training in a given event, were decided. This was all done with the needs of the particular style of The Fox Hotel, and the needs of its particular guests, in mind. The interventions (indicated by the small stars) are opportunities for reviewing and criticizing what has just been done in an event. They are also for looking ahead at what will have to be done in the event which follows.

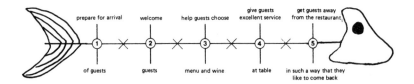

Figure 7 *The S-R events in a training course for waiters.*

Use your intuition, creativity and logical thinking to fill in some of the stimuli (S) — materials, content of films or content of role-playing — which you would use in one of the didactical events along the fishbone. What are some of the responses (R) for learning you would want the trainee waiters to make in the event you have chosen? Ask yourself why those particular responses are so important.

If you can't get going, start the vibrations going in your think tank by thinking of some 'incidents' which it would be important to handle in this course: a guest spills wine over the table; a waiter spills wine over a guest(!); a guest cannot pay her bill . . . . Let the fishbone model work for you as your referent 3.

When you have more time, choose a subject that you know and would like to teach — playing chess, stopping nosebleeds,

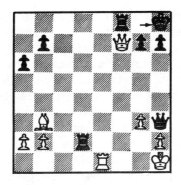

mending a bicycle tyre — it doesn't matter what it is. Think about the 'needs' in terms of the end goal, and so on. Let an initial idea form in your mind about how you are going to teach it. Think about some existing design which could help you find a design. Let this existing design interact with your initial idea for a design. Do you notice their influence on each other? If you do, you are experiencing referent 3: an appropriate model, at work.

Referent 4: A response environment organizer

Sometimes in thinking up a design, you can have the best didactical intention (referent 1) in mind, your specification or databank (referent 2) filled with the right needs, an existing design (referent 3) sending out interesting signals, and yet you are still waiting — waiting for that 'click' as the parts of the puzzle fall into place and your decision-making goes racing and tumbling to its conclusion.

referent 4

There *is* something which can make this happen, something which will accelerate the 'click'; a cunning designer is always watching and listening for it. It is a 'bit of content' which has two quite unique properties for the designer using it. The first is that, in the presence of referents 1, 2 and 3, it triggers a picture in the designer's mind of what the teaching—learning situation is going to be. The second is that it clearly has the potential (as it joins the rest of the content in the course or lesson) to serve as an anchor point and stimulator of the students' learning. Its choice and use will do much in deciding how effective, valued, liked and efficient the learning experience is going to be. The 'special bit of content' is referent 4: an effective response environment organizer, or for short, an effective REO. In case study 1, the special bit of content which gave the vision of the designed encounter, with its pre- and post- visit programmes, was the visualized five-element concept of general practice shown in Fig. 2, page 22. With its arrival, the pieces of the puzzle fell into place.

Scrutinize closely any description of a course or lesson that has scored highly on the *Emax Vmax Lmax E'max* criteria. In 99 cases out of 100 you will find an effective response environment organizer operating for the student in the way described above. It is also safe to speculate that its presence enabled the teacher or designer to 'see' how she or he was going to set up the learning experience of the student. Bits of content which I know personally (or have been told about) that have been used successfully as an effective referent 4 include: 'eleven words on a blackboard', 'a set of symbols', 'a piece of sculpture', 'a curious medical symptom', 'a poem by D H Lawrence', 'Vincent Van Gogh's small canvas: *meadow grass*', 'a hay fork', 'the sounds of a patient's heartbeats', 'the contents of a letter written by a Consul in Jerusalem to his superiors in Rome'. Special bits of content are used intuitively by good teachers as the nucleus of courses and lessons. They have been in the tool kits of gifted teachers for a very, very long time.

Below is a description by a writer (Bruner, 1966) who is recalling his own learning experience, and by implication that of his fellow students, in a series of lectures on the subject of literary appreciation. The *special bit of content* which determined the students' appreciation of the course is the 'eleven words on the blackboard'. The eleven words are functioning (for the teacher and learner) as a response environment organizer.

As a student, I took a course with I A Richards ... It began with that extraordinary teacher turning his back to the class and writing on the blackboard in his sharply angular hand the lines:

> Gray is all theory
> Green grows the golden tree of life.

For three weeks we stayed with the lines, with the imagery of the classic and romantic views, with the critics who had sought to explore the two ways of life; we became involved in reading a related but bad play of Goethe's, *Torquato Tasso*, always in a state of dialogue though Richards alone spoke. The reading time for eleven words was three weeks. It was the antithesis of just reading, and the reward in the end was that I owned outright, free and clear, eleven words. A good bargain. Never before had I read with such a lively sense of conjecture, like a speaker and not a listener, or like a writer and not a reader.

Jerome S Bruner (1966) *Toward a Theory of Instruction*
With permission: Harvard University Press.

It is apparent that the eleven words on the blackboard, in the hands of this gifted teacher, served very clearly as the organizer of the students' learning experience — an experience which the writer and his fellow students found to be of superlative quality. We can also safely conjecture that when these eleven words (from Goethe) crossed the teacher's path, he was able to say: 'Eureka! Now I *see* how I must give my course!' It was his special bit of content for a successful design.

Referent 4, for a given piece of instruction, is discovered, invented, or meticulously constructed by the designer-teacher, or by the designer when, for example, a teacher is not involved. My own criteria for deciding that a bit of content is an effective REO, ie an effective referent 4, are these:

☐ the bit of content is a 'system of stimuli', that has the capacity — via the stimuli it contains — of generating the responses needed to shape the student's learning to the instructional goals that have been set in an interesting and meaningful way.

☐ the bit of content can migrate, so to speak, quite naturally into the design itself, and become the focal point of the student's learning experience.

☐ the bit of content must serve as what Ausubel and Robinson (1961) have referred to as an 'anchoring idea' or 'organizer' in the cognitive structure of the learner that facilitates learning.

☐ the bit of content is chosen, invented or constructed with the other three referents in mind: a set of criteria for a good design (referent 1), the nth specification of the needs (referent 2), and an appropriate model (referent 3).

☐ the bit of content that the designer is contemplating as her or his response environment organizer (in the presence of the other three referents and the emerging idea of a design) generates, for the designer using it, an insight into the teaching/learning situation that is needed to realize the learning goals that have been set. In short, the bit of content in question (in the presence of the other referents) is the precursor in the designer's thinking of the design *per se*.

A *response environment organizer* is a very personal thing. A bit of content serving one designer as referent 4 is not necessarily an effective referent 4 for another designer who is designing a course on the same subject for the same students and with the same goals in mind. The Goethe quotation, for example, is a very personal use of a quotation. It may very well not function as an REO for another teacher of literary appreciation. He or she would need to discover, invent or meticulously construct his or her own REO. Referent 4 is the product of one's own intuition, creativity and logical thinking.

Here's an exercise in the use of REOs. Go back for a moment into your think tank with the problem of deciding what is a good design for lessons on teaching six-year-olds to tell the time.

Can you think of a special bit of content that would serve you as an effective referent 4? If you have one, do you notice how this item sends changes chasing through the items in your databank (referent 2)? Does the special bit of content, if you have it, help your design pass the test of the criteria for a good design (referent 1)? Did or could the bit of content come from some existing design (referent 3) that you know about? If you don't have an REO, is perhaps a shadow of an REO emerging?

The bit of content which is dancing around in my think tank at the moment (together with sundials, boiled eggs, cuckoo clocks, moons, digital twelve-hour-watches, birthday cakes with candles, and calendars) is the special time, on a 24-hour digital clock with a display of hours, minutes and seconds: 12   12   12. With the help of this time and the things mentioned, I can let the six-year-olds:

1. experience that there is a difference between 'one year', 'one day', '24 hours', '12 hours', 'half a day', '12 minutes' and '12 seconds',
2. learn the difference between a digital watch and a conventional watch,
3. know that an alarm going off at '12' can be at 12 o'clock in the day or 12 o'clock at night, and
4. actually 'experience', by boiling an egg, the difference between an egg that has been boiled for 12 minutes, for 12 seconds and for 12 hours.

By using 12   12   12, I can also teach the children not to become 'slaves' of the hours, minutes and seconds of the day. With its help, we can even begin to explore the question, 'What *is* time?'. We can make sense of the quarters in a year and the path of the moon . . . .

Referent 4 was our last referent in the four-referent paradigm proposed in this book. The referents are decision-making tools to help you transform a problem situation into a solution situation. In the privacy of your mind you *know* what 'plan, structure and strategy of instruction' you are going to use. The next step is to give this concept — still an abstract notion in your mind — concrete form. You must now work out this thought-up design. After a case study describing a design problem and its solution, you will meet some tips for use when thinking up a design. After that we will go on to Chapter 3 and the task of working out a thought-up design.

Before you begin reading case study no. 2, refresh your memory of the names of the four referents by turning back to Fig. 3 on page 33.

Case study no. 2: Fighting forest fires safely

On repeated occasions in 1964 on the shuttle flight between La Guardia airport New York and National airport Washington DC,

I was struggling with a course design problem. It seemed relatively simple and yet the solution (the choice of a plan, structure and strategy of instruction for the course involved) eluded me time and time again.

At the time I was assigned by the consulting company for which I worked in New York to an account in the US Forestry Service (Fire Control Division) in Washington DC. The service was concerned about the loss of life and injury to personnel that had occurred in some large forest fires in the western states of America. A directive on the subject, formulated years earlier,

was re-issued for urgent attention. The directive was crystal clear. It referred to *Ten Safety Orders* for strict observance when fighting forest fires. 'These orders', the directive ran, 'are to be committed to memory by all personnel with fire control responsibility'. The directive to me was also unequivocal: 'Go to Washington, work with the US Forestry Service Training Department (Bert Holtby) and with the Fire Control Division (John Pierovich) and make an effective, valued (etc) course to teach the ten orders.' The orders which had to be taught have already been listed in Chapter 1, ie:

1. Keep informed on fire weather conditions and forecasts.
2. Know what your fire is doing at all times.
3. Base all actions on current and expected behaviour of fire.
4. Have escape routes for everyone and make them known.
5. Post lookouts when there is possible danger.
6. Be alert, keep calm, think clearly, act decisively.
7. Maintain prompt communications with your men, your boss and adjoining forces.
8. Give clear instructions and be sure they are understood.
9. Maintain control of your men at all times.
10. Fight fire aggressively but provide for safety first.

What design to use? The question went round and round and round in my head.

The sixties were the days of 'programmed instruction'. We had the equivalent of this book's criteria for a good design in mind — active not passive learning, critical use of media and so on. We wanted to score well against the *Emax Vmax Lmax E' max* formula. This was important and challenging. The population to be trained were very varied in their attitude to ways of learning and in what each group found important. Professional fire fighters especially needed to value the method of learning; they were frontline operations men. Forest Rangers (also in the population) and volunteer fire fighters had their special preferences too. The need was clear, and at the end of training the 'ten safety orders' had to be known and the importance of their application in a real situation appreciated.

Referent 2 was, thus, ready made for us. (See Figure 5, p. 39.) The trainees involved had to know the ten orders — this was the 'end goal' in our databank. The 'success criteria' had to be some sort of successful performance in an end test which tested for recall of the orders. The 'content' in the course was the content of the ten safety orders themselves. The 'method', in view of the fact that training had to be decentralised, had to be the self-study method of programmed instruction; the 'media' was to be the printed word. The 'constraints' were our greatest challenge: the trainee population was a heterogeneous one, scattered throughout the American continent and Puerto Rico; the orders (worded and numbered as shown) could not be changed in any way — even to facilitate learning.

The most we had in the form of a referent 3 (an appropriate model) was our familiarity with the strategy and format of any programmed instruction text. No specific design for teaching safety orders successfully via a programmed text was known to us. With all these givens, we still had no design. Not one, at least, which would satisfy the criteria for a good design (referent 1). By now we were some one hundred, relatively costly, man-hours into the project...

The first break-through came on a Washington to New York flight after a meeting with the Fire Control Division staff. I must have studied the Ten Safety Orders 40 times or more, but decided to have one more look. In retrospect (in the terms of the paradigm given in this book) I was looking for that special bit of content — a response environment organizer.

I didn't find it. What I *did* find, and wondered why I hadn't noticed it sooner, was a 'system' in the orders. It was a system which made it possible to split up the orders into three subsets with safety order number 10 standing apart from the other nine as the 'alpha and omega' in fighting a forest fire: *Fight fire aggressively but provide for safety first*. It came to be called the $\alpha\Omega$ order in the finished course. The system in the orders, with the subsets named in a way that would help eventually teach them, is given in Fig. 8.

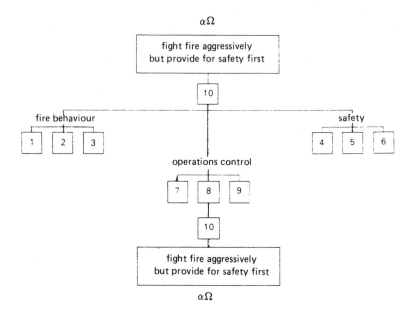

Figure 8 *A helpful didactical grouping of the 10 safety orders.*

With the splitting up of the orders into their inherent subsets (orders number 1, 2 and 3 relating to fire behaviour, orders 4, 5 and 6 to safety, and orders 7, 8 and 9 to operations control), we had a didactically useful ordering of the course content. But we still had no design . . .

We were by now something like three man-weeks into the project.

Finally, '*it*' came. I was lunching with John Pierovich from the Fire Control Division. He mentioned that he had to attend an enquiry in the afternoon over a fire fighting operation in which lives had been lost and individuals injured. My intuition prompted me to ask him more. Amongst my questions was, 'How do you run such an enquiry?'. He explained that the debriefing of the personnel who had been at the scene of the fire was done with the help of 'fire situation maps'. For me that was the 'click'. Some hours later we were poring over examples of such maps. A specific situation was given in schematic form: symbols representing firebreaks which were (at the time of the disaster) in the making, the type of terrain in which the fire was being fought, the wind direction and velocity, the location of spot fires which had broken out and had been started by burning debris carried in the wind, and so on. An example of such a map is shown in Fig. 9.

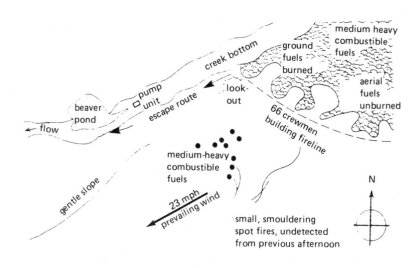

Figure 9 *A fire situation map.*

Well, you have probably guessed the rest. The content of five carefully chosen fire situation maps (some of them modified to suit the teaching need) was our *response environment organizer*. Combined with the schema (Fig. 8) and the notion of the alpha-omega safety order, we had a design. Some five man-weeks later the self-study text (Earl et al, 1964) and accompanying maps for analysis exercises were ready for testing in the field. From the initial reaction in the Forestry Service and Fire Control Division

I think it is correct to say that we could be satisfied with what we had made.

The type of inductive/deductive thinking which the design used to teach the 'ten safety orders' can be illustrated with the help of the map given in Fig. 10, and two frames (Fig. 11) from a sequence of frames in the programmed text which related to this particular map.

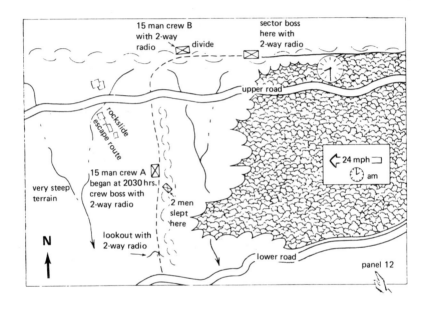

Figure 10 *Panel 12 from the programmed text.*

In the programme, the map is called a 'panel'. It was numbered panel 12. A 'frame' was the name given to a small unit of information to which the reader of a programmed text would be asked to respond. The correct response was revealed only after the reader had responded. Ten such frames (see Figure 11) were used in the programme in an analysis of the particular fire fighting situation depicted in panel 12 (see Figure 10).

The design of a sequence such as you see in Fig. 11 makes the learner do several things:

1. analyse what she or he sees

PROGRAM   1087   FRAME NO.   173   CORRECT RESPONSE

REFER TO PANEL 12

What means of communications can you conclude
were established between sector boss and crew boss?

_____   2-way radio

Between lookout and crew boss? _____   2-way radio

Between crew boss and crewmen?_____   word-of-mouth

How about between crewmen themselves?   by keeping in contact
_____   through word-of-mouth

With crew B? _____   2-way radio

Communication conformed to Fire Order 7
which says:

7 _____   MAINTAIN PROMPT
  _____   COMMUNICATIONS
  _____   WITH YOUR MEN,
                                                        YOUR BOSS AND
                                                        ADJOINING FORCES

PROGRAM   1087   FRAME NO.   174   CORRECT RESPONSE

STILL REFER TO PANEL 12

At 0200 hrs (2:00 am) the fire was sent racing
towards the planned control line by an unexpected
increase in wind speed to   mph.   24

The crew boss orderd the men off the fire line. This
order was given:

'Drop tools — go back up-line
and west along the road to the
big rockslide. 1 squad boss lead
on — the rest follow — I'll bring
up the rear."

Would you say that the crew boss
Would you say that the crew boss had complied   yes
with Fire Order 8? ☐ yes ☐ no   Fire Order 8 requires you
                                                     to "Give clear instruction
EXPLAIN (briefly). _____   and make sure they are
                                                     understood." By using a
_____   squad boss to lead the
                                                     way and by bringing up
_____   the rear he made sure his
                                                     orders were understood.
_____
                                                     (or equivalent response)

Figure 11 *Frames 173 and 174 from the programmed text.*

2. recall the relevant safety order
3. evaluate whether or not an order has been complied with in a real-life situation.

It was important that the design worked this way for a heterogeneous population of learners and a critical group of learners from out of the field.

Years later, I was working in Europe, the fire fighting course-making was an interesting experience in the past, when I had a nice surprise. By pure chance I met a forest fire fighter from the USA in a bar in Amsterdam. He knew the course; he had learned from it and had liked it. We toasted, I remember, the Forestry Service, the USA, the Netherlands and the course several times. This seemed a good ending to the search for a design which started on a flight out of New York to Washington DC some four years earlier.

Some tips

1. Find a big wall or a big sheet of paper and draw the diagram in Fig. 3, page 33.

2. Write in big, bold letters under your diagram:
   YOU WORK FOR ME, NOT ME FOR YOU!

3. Stand on one leg and repeat three times: 'I'm intuitive, I'm creative, I can think logically'.

4. Find a very quiet place (a place you like) and think about the students you are going to teach tomorrow, or next week, or next month, or whenever. Think about their intellectual, emotional, spiritual and physical quadrants.

5. Learn this definition by heart: 'A responsive environment organizer is a special bit of content (a system of stimuli) capable, in the hands of the designer using it, of generating the responses needed to shape the student's learning to the instructional goals that have been set, in an interesting and meaningful way'.

6. If you are ever in a taxi in New York, explain briefly to the driver what an REO is. Ask him or her for an REO for a course in training New York taxi drivers to be good NY drivers.

7. Talk to yourself about the fishbone model (Fig. 6, page 41).

8. As a designer: *think clearly, act decisively, but provide for safety first.*

Chapter 3
Working Out a Design

Introduction

'What is the difference between the mental gymnastics of
thinking up a design and the mental gymnastics of working out
a design?'

The question took me by surprise. It came from a teacher on
the second day of a Think Tank workshop in Friedberg, West
Germany. It took me by surprise because until then I had never

really given much thought to the difference or about how to
make the difference clear. The teacher who asked the question
waited for an answer. I had to find it quickly. My answer was:
'In thinking up a design, the design is responding to *you*. In
working one out, you are responding to *it*'.

Essentially, this would still be my answer were I asked the
same question today. As you switch to the mental gymnastics
of working out a design, the design begins to 'talk' to you. It
begins to demand things: 'Make me an exercise for testing the
students' understanding of the Tyndall effect'; 'Make me a video
tape that will let the learner experience the genius of Van Gogh';
'Get hold of a water diviner who can demonstrate his skill with
a hazel stick'; 'Make an overview of the course so the student
knows where she or he is going'; 'Introduce the special bit

of content that is going to be the student's REO at the very beginning of the course and not bit-by-bit'; 'Collect...'; 'Copy...'; 'Translate ...'. When the time comes to work out the design you have thought up, it will keep you very busy!

After the Friedberg workshop incident, I decided to give more attention in the workshops to the task of working out a thought-up design. This wasn't so easy. There was relatively little time to work out designs. Working out a design meant writing materials, making diagrams, selecting concepts, putting things together, preparing teaching aids and so on. I had a design problem myself!

After talking to myself for quite a long time about how best to handle the subject of working out a design in the workshop in a *meaningful* way, I drew a diagram. I had to practice what I preached about meaningful responding. The content of the diagram became the special bit of content for explaining the process of working out a design and for distinguishing this process from the process of thinking up a design. The diagram is given in Fig. 12.

With the content of Fig. 12 as an anchor point for learning, it was possible to analyse worked-out designs and pin-point some important facets of setting up S-R events. This was done with the help of worked-out designs for subjects as diverse as

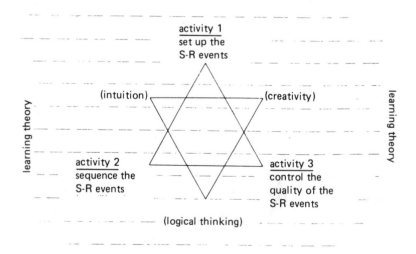

Figure 12 *The things involved in working out a design.*

'picking a lock', 'reading a balance sheet', 'avoiding conflict in a ticketing situation', 'escaping from a car under water', 'buying meat', 'baking bagels', 'boring a hole', 'treating a snake bite' and 'stopping nosebleeds'. We also didn't miss the golden chance of analysing the worked-out design of the workshop itself. This was a 'living example', and a good teacher.

Working out a design involves the three activities given in Fig. 12. The thought-up design is at the centre, directing the operation, but leaving room for your intuition, creativity and logical thinking. From time to time you will need to make an excursion to learning theory. This will be with a specific question, which will demand a concrete answer, eg, 'What has learning theory to say about the role of fear when fighting a fire?', 'Can children of six handle this abstract notion about time?', 'What is the best way of dividing a class of students into work groups?'.

If the thought-up design in your think tank is a good one it will be vibrating with energy and wanting to be worked out. You will like working for it!

What does setting up the S-R events involve?

An S-R event is an educational happening. It has a beginning, a middle and an end. It occupies a relatively short or relatively long time-slot in the course or lesson to which it belongs. It has its own identity. If necessary you can, for example, temporarily take it out of the course or lesson, clean up any elements in it that are giving trouble, and put it back again. An exercise in problem-solving, a laboratory demonstration, a class discussion of a controversial topic, a lecture, and an educational visit to a jam factory, are all examples of an S-R event.

Up to the moment of working out a design, you have seen the content and activities in the events suggested by the design only as brief, often fleeting, images in the video of your mind. In thinking up a design you must not, in fact, be concerned with detail.

In the task of giving these images concrete (detailed) form, it can be useful to recognise four types of S-R event (Table 4). The first type are events which have to instruct. The second are events which have to explain. The third are events which tell something, and finally, the fourth type are events which let the learner encounter something.

Table 4: *Four types of S-R event*

A	B	C	D
to instruct	to instruct	to instruct	to instruct
to explain	*to explain*	to explain	to explain
to tell	to tell	*to tell*	to tell
to let encounter	to let encounter	to let encounter	*to let encounter*

The S-R events in the best courses and lessons have elements of instruction, explaining, telling, and letting encounter in them. This is important for a good *Emax Vmax Lmax E'max* score. One of these four elements will be the primary goal of the event and will indicate to which type, A or B or C or D, it belongs. Knowing to which type the S-R event you are setting up belongs is essential when you are giving concrete form to a thought-up design.

On conclusion of an event which has to *instruct*, the student must be able to *do* something which he or she was not able to do at the start. An event which has to instruct has a behavioural objective. If, for example, you are a policeman or woman in Amsterdam, the chances are that you have been instructed in

the use of protocol such as is seen in Table 5. This protocol can be followed when you see a moving or stationary traffic violation. It is designed to minimize the chance of conflict between you and the person involved. At the end of the S-R event you would be able to demonstrate your knowledge of the steps in the protocol and be able to apply them in a test situation.

An S-R event which has to *explain* has the responsibility of giving meaning to something. It could be, for example, that in the police training course mentioned above an explanation had to be given of how to react when a traffic-rule violator refuses to give her or his name to the officer. If you have been in an S-R event in which something has been well explained, you will,

Table 5: *A protocol for use in a ticketing situation*

---

1. Decide your end goal.
2. Bring to a halt.
3. Open interaction.
4. Give citizen room to react.
5. Make rebuttal.
6. Establish identity.
7. Gather further particulars.

---

on exiting from that event, be able to explain to somebody else what has been explained to you.

Events which have to *tell* have the responsibility of informing the learner about something. The best of these (those whose message you remember long after the event is over) will certainly have the other elements of explanation, instruction and encounter in them.

Some of our richest learning moments are in *encounters*. These are the S-R events in which you are confronted with something to which you are invited to respond in your personal, individual, way. An educational encounter has an end goal but that end goal is never directive. In the police course, the police trainees encounter escalation on the streets of Amsterdam in a series of video films. They experience through filmed incidents what sort of things to expect when issuing a ticket for a traffic violation. They react to these incidents in their individual way — both in the privacy of their minds and, later, openly in a discussion with their fellow trainees.

Take a few moments to talk to yourself about *instructing* someone on what to do when bitten in the ankle by a poisonous snake. Theoretically, the first thing is to restrict the flow of blood to and from the affected limb. The next is cut into the area of the bite with a clean, sharp instrument and suck out the

poison. The third is to pass on critical information and get the appropriate medical help. Snake bite kits are available: would you use one as part of the instruction? What would you think is 'critical information' in this context? How quick must you be in doing what has to be done? What sort of end test would tell you that the S-R event you have in mind has instructed? Isn't it dangerous to suck snake poison into your mouth? Are all snake bites dangerous? How does the poison work? Anti-serum is produced with the help of a horse: why a horse? An S-R event which has to instruct you in treating a snake bite has lots of things to explain, tell, and let you encounter. It can score highly against the *Emax Vmax Lmax E'max* formula.

What choice is there for sequencing the S-R events?

'Chain', 'necklace', 'spiral', 'network', 'hybrid' — these are the titles we use in the Think Tank workshop for the different methods of sequencing S-R events that a thought-up design can demand. A thought-up design has a 'route map' in it; it will tell you the order in which it wants the worked-out design to let the learner meet the content (substance) of the course or lesson.

The chain

The *chain* is a sequence in which the various S-R events in a procedure which is being taught are built around each step in that procedure or process.

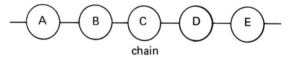

chain

Treating a snake bite, for example, would be a procedure to be taught in a chain. The protocol for police ticketing situations could also be sequenced for learning as a chain of events. The steps in a chain can be, and usually are, taught in their natural order — A, then B, then C, and so on. This is known as a *forward chain*. It is also possible (and sometimes extremely effective) to teach the steps in *reverse* order. This would mean teaching the last step first and working backwards until the first step in the chain is reached. Do you remember the example of the waiter-training design mentioned in Chapter 2? This was a chain of events which could very well be taught by starting with an S-R event on the subject of 'getting guests away from the restaurant in such a way that they like to come back'. The last S-R event to be taught would then be on the subject of 'preparing for the arrival of the guests'. Try thinking of some other subjects which could be successfully taught by sequencing them in a backward chain. Examples which come up in the Think Tank workshop include 'selling oil', 'solving a problem', 'playing a piece of music' and 'tying a shoelace'.

The necklace

Some processes are cyclical in nature. When you have to teach them in a course or lesson the sequence to use is the closed chain or *necklace* sequence. The example of a worked-out design in necklace sequence that we use in the Think Tank

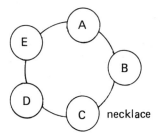

necklace

workshop is for a course on solving a food problem in a Third World country. The course is for young biologists. Its goal is to teach (with the help of case studies, talks by experts, discussions, films and exercises) a systematic approach to solving a country's food shortage problem. The steps in this strategy are given in Fig. 13.

This is the 'special bit of content' which works as the REO in the worked-out version of the course. This worked-out design has had success. It is well valued and liked and rated positively in terms of being effective and also efficient.

The spiral

A *spiral* sequence is an alternative sequence to those already mentioned; it will result in a worked-out design in which the same topics are covered two, three or even more times. Each time the round of topics is made, each topic is handled in its S-R event at a progressively higher level of complexity and at a greater depth. The spiral sequence can be used (with the help

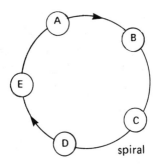

spiral

of intuition, creativity and logical thinking) in courses and lessons on subjects from a list that is practically endless; arithmetic, economics, computer science, product processing in milk factories, art history, strategies in chess, building a house, statistics, and the scientific method of enquiry are just a few of these. A thought-up design could also make you spiral downwards (from the complex to the simple) when it gets you to work it out.

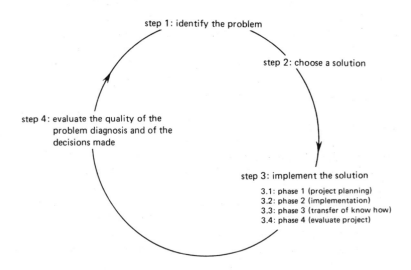

Figure 13 *A problem-solving strategy (food development project).*

The network

'How much is to be borrowed?', 'What is the loan to be used for?', 'What are the repayment plans?', 'What will be the bank's position if repayment plans fail?'... If you have ever studied the design of a course for bankers on negotiating cash loans to companies, you will be aware that its S-R events will handle

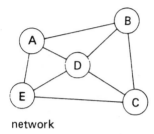

network

questions like these. One or other event is also likely to handle the separate subjects of insuring cash loans, and reading a balance sheet. You will find that the topics and subjects in the course are such that there is no advantage in sequencing the S-R events in a chain or necklace. Instead, the S-R events are put together in a *network*. The events relate to each other. They complement each other, but one S-R event does not in principle have to precede or follow another event. A modularized learning system (in which the student chooses her or his own route through the different S-R events that make up the system) is a network of S-R events. The choice of sequencing the S-R events is, in principle, an *arbitrary* one.

The hybrid

'A blood-soaked handkerchief, tissues or towels... a frightened patient with one or more friends or relatives in near panic...' These are the opening lines in an article (Norman, 1970) for doctors on the subject of nosebleeds and how to handle them in the local surgery. We use the article and the information in it in the Think Tank workshop. It is an excellent subject for an exercise in hybrid sequencing. A *hybrid* sequence, as the name suggests, is a mixed sequence: some of the S-R events are sequenced in, for example, a network, and some in a chain; or some in a spiral and some in a network. In a course for doctors on 'handling nosebleeds', the clinical procedure involved can be taught as a chain. This is the 'know how' part of the course.

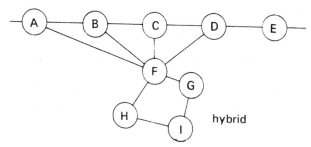

The 'know what' part, covering important anatomical information and the physiological implications of a nosebleed, can
be taught via a network of S-R events. With the help of this
subject we learn how to work out a hybrid sequence and also to
value this particular sequence as a means of bringing variety in
the sequencing of a course or lesson. Variety is something that
learners always like.

What does 'controlling the quality of an S-R event' involve?

This activity in the working out of a design is something which
is going on intuitively and automatically when you have had
some experience in working out designs. This is because, as you
come to work out a thought-up design, the criteria for a good
design which helped you think it up have taken on an im-
perative ring. In thinking up a design, criterion 1, for example,
said that 'a good design generates an active (not passive) learning
situation'. It now gives the command: 'Generate an active
(not passive) learning experience.' Criterion 2, which said that
'a good design utilizes didactically meaningful responses and
excludes non-meaningful responses', now gives the command:
'Utilize didactically meaningful responses and exclude non-
meaningful responses.' The remaining criteria now command
you to:

☐ Criterion 3: Exercise the appropriate degree of control over
the learning process.
☐ Criterion 4: Respect but outwit constraints.
☐ Criterion 5: Provide the learner with feedback.
☐ Criterion 6: Make critical use of media.
☐ Criterion 7: Extend as needed.
☐ Criterion 8: Base your decision on the specified needs.

As your decision-making shifts to working out a design and you begin to use the criteria for a good design, *you* begin to work *for them*.

Would you like to exercise your understanding of these criteria and their importance when working out a design? If you would, take the time to look for the influence of the criteria in the descriptions of worked-out designs in the two case studies which follow. You will find that these criteria are certainly helping control the quality of S-R events, while never telling you *how* to work out a design. This is something your intuition, creativity, and logical thinking have to do as you respond to the directives from the design you have thought up and must now work out.

Case study no. 3: Pictures in your mind

From our own experience in learning situations we know how special and important it can be to imagine something. Why then don't we (as designers and teachers) give more attention to the use of the student's imagination in a teaching-learning situation? Imagination can be a very powerful tool for learning. Below is a description of an S-R event in which didactic use is being deliberately made of a doctor's imagination. It is one event in a network of events in a course on dermatology. The REO for the course is a phrase from a book entitled *Read the Skin* (Merck, 1979). It sprang out at me from a page of the book as I educated myself enough on the subject of dermatology to understand the needs of the learners, who were general practitioners. The phrase is: 'Recognize, assess significance for the patient, initiate appropriate treatment'. It contains the quintessence of good medical practice in the area of dermatology, and became the leitmotiv that runs through the network of events in the course.

The S-R event described below is S-R event number 4 in the course. It is an exercise in a self-study text (Earl and Luttik, 1983) which was recommended for study prior to group discussions on dermatological cases which the participants had met in their own practices. The S-R event is taken verbatim from the self-study text.

Pictures in your mind

Conjure up in your mind a mental picture of the three skin problems named below. As you think about each, formulate an

65

answer to three questions:

1. How would you recognize the condition, ie what are its characteristics?
2. What could its significance be for the patient — clinically, psychologically and socially?
3. What treatment, if any, would you be thinking about?

In each case assume that the patient's decision to ask or come for help is a wise one. The condition is already well advanced.

☐ *Problem 1:* Acne vulgaris (15-year-old girl)
☐ *Problem 2:* 'Housewife's hands' (a busy, 34-year-old mother with three children under five years old)
☐ *Problem 3:* Erysipelas (45-year-old teacher. His wife is so alarmed at his appearance that she asks you to make a house call as quickly as possible)

Make short notes for each problem under the appropriate headings.

P.1. Acne Vulgaris. RECOGNITION: ....

....

SIGNIFICANCE FOR PATIENT:.........................

....

TREATMENT: ....

....

....

(*Note:* Short notes are also invited in this format for Problem 2: 'Housewife's Hands', and Problem 3: Erysipelas.)

Critical feedback information is provided for the learner in the form of notes on these skin disorders and their recognition, significance and treatment. These have been put together by a general practitioner who knows the work situation of the learners, and a dermatologist with specialized knowledge.

Can you recognize how active responding (criterion 1), meaningful responding (criterion 2), assignment of control of the learning process to the reader (criterion 3), outwitting constraints relating to individual states of knowledge (criterion 4), provision of feedback (criterion 5) and shaping of the form and content of the event to the needs of a specific learner population (criterion 8), are cared for in the design of this S-R event? If necessary, further diseases could also be added for 'imaging' and comment in this exercise. It could be extended with relative ease (criterion 7). Critical use of media (criterion 6) can be recognized in the use of pictures which the learner must conjure up in her or his own mind.

Case study no. 4: Giving students the chance to think for themselves

As a designer of courses and lessons you will always be in demand if you have success in creating response environments for learning in which students are given the responsibility and the chance to think for themselves. This was the case a few years ago when two teachers (P. Schildwacht and C. Papenhuyzen) from the Department of Botany at the University of Utrecht, Netherlands, came to our department (the Department of Research and Development in Education) seeking help in designing

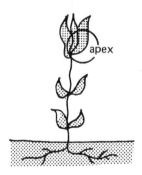

a five-day experiment in which their students could investigate and think about a phenomenon in plants known as 'apical dominance'. This has to do with the fact that the bud at the apex of certain plants grows much faster and more luxuriously than buds down the stem. It occurs despite the fact that the apical bud is least favourably situated in respect to access to nutrients in the soil. The phenomenon has interested scientists for a long time. It still does.

The teachers seeking assistance were responding to a complaint from students that they had too many prescriptive type experiments in their curriculum. These are experiments in

67

which the student works from a step-by-step protocol and is given little opportunity to work and think in her or his own way. The teachers were willing to convert their protocol-steered experiment into a think-and-do-for-yourself type experiment. They needed help in doing this. There were 65 students involved and it was difficult to visualize them working effectively on their own, without the sort of help a protocol was able to give them. A colleague (P.J. van Eijl) and I were asked to respond to the teachers' call for help.

It wasn't very long before the five steps in the so-called 'scientific method of enquiry' began to attract attention as the special bit of content which would serve as the students' response environment organizer. It was intuitively seen as the most natural REO in a think-and-do-for-yourself scientific

observe phenomenon
make an hypothesis
make a work hypothesis
test hypothesis
draw conclusions

experiment. The challenge was how to weave it into place in a didactic design so that the design would be experienced not only as valued and liked but also effective and efficient for a group of 65 individuals with different interests and skills. It was quite a challenge!

Finally, a design emerged. Some fifteen working days into the project we saw how it had to be. The steps in the scientific method (observing the phenomenon, formulating a general hypothesis, formulating a work hypothesis, testing the work hypothesis, and drawing conclusions) were made the focal point of five S-R events. These were supported by 11 other S-R events. Seven of these were discussions between the teacher and the students on what they had just done and what they were about to do. The S-R events were sequenced into a chain. The design split the 65 students into seven groups of seven and two groups of eight. It assigned an experienced teacher or an assistant teacher to the role of mentor in each group. The design in its worked-out form contained the 16 S-R events listed in Fig. 14. These S-R events involved individual (I) activity, group (G) activity and teacher intervention (T) activity (see Fig. 14).

1. *Observe Phenomenon* (I) (G)
2. Discussion (I) (G) (T)
3. Focus on apical dominance (I) (G)
4. *Formulate general hypothesis* (I) (G)
5. Discussion (I) (G) (T)
6. *Formulate work hypothesis* (I) (G)
7. Discussion (I) (G) (T)
8. Design experiment (I) (G)
9. Discussion (I) (G) (T)
10. *Test-work hypothesis* (I) (G)
11. Discussion (I) (G) (T)
12. *Draw conclusions* (I) (G)
13. Discussion (I) (G) (T)
14. Write report (I) (G)
15. Discussion/evaluation of report (I) (G) (T)
16. Exchange of results between groups (I) (G) (T)

Figure 14 *The S-R events in a think-and-do-for-yourself type experiment.*

The activities included reading, looking, discriminating, judging, discussing, completion of experimental formulae, steering of the process, and so on. This reflects care for active and not passive learning (criterion 1). The discussion events provided the chance to look back at and evaluate the quality of the activities and decisions which had just been made. They also provided the opportunity to look forward at what was intended in the event which followed. This feedback reflects concern for criterion 5. It came (in a non-directive way) from the teacher of the group and also from members of the group themselves.

To ensure that the individual student and the groups of students could respond in a didactically meaningful way (criterion 2) to what was asked of them, *help stimuli* were provided for use in each event. In S-R event 6, for example, these help stimuli were in the form of a set of criteria for a good working hypothesis. They were also in the form of a list of references and a selection of important current information and theories on the subject of apical dominance. Without these, the students involved did not have enough basic knowledge and experience to formulate a working hypothesis that would satisfy the scrutiny of the group teacher and (perhaps) fellow students.

The splitting of the students into groups of seven and eight allowed the design to share control over the learning process (criterion 3) between students as individuals, and between the group and the teacher. Working as individuals and as a group also helped outwit existing constraints (criterion 4), which included too many students, too little time, and limited laboratory resources.

Once the thought-up design had been worked out, it was time to test it before its formal installation in the Botany curriculum as a regular laboratory experiment (new style) on the phenomenon of apical dominance.

The results of the first try-out were not exactly as anticipated. We were happy enough to discover that in the main, all groups valued and liked the new think-and-do-for-yourself type experiment. Reactions as to how effective and efficient the experiment was were mixed. The results, as scored against the *Emax Vmax Lmax E'max* criteria, were for some groups $E \mp V + L + E' \mp$, and for other groups $E \pm V + L + E' \pm$. What could account for these differences? The results are certainly worth improving. How? The opinion of the teachers and assistants on the new method of experiment came out about the same: practically all valued and liked the change from the prescriptive form of experiment, but not all found it effective and efficient. What they did say was that they had never had to work so hard before in assigning and supervizing a laboratory task. But they all thought it worthwhile! This was a healthy signal to the design group.

The teaching-learning situation described above is an *encounter* with the scientific method of enquiry. *Telling* and *explaining* came through the materials which served as helping stimuli in the different events. *Instruction* touched the learning experience during the discussions with the laboratory teacher and during *ad hoc* teacher intervention when help was asked for at the laboratory bench.

The above results are reasonably good but there is room for some revisions. What do you think these revisions might be? What factors are interfering with the experiment's success?

We'll come back to this diagnosis at the end of Chapter 4, on testing-and-revising a thought-up, worked-out design. In the meantime you may like to think of an answer to these questions yourself or together with another reader of this book.

Some tips

1. As you work out a design, think now and again of exciting a learner response in an unusual way: listening to silence; reading a 'difficult to read' text by starting with the last chapter; mentally practising a manual operation with the eyes closed.

2. Be very suspicious of the quality of an explanation (written or verbal) when you find yourself using the word 'thus'. Your 'thus' is not necessarily the learner's 'thus'!

3. If someone wonders (as they frequently do) why it took so long to think up and work out a design, have the following thought (Gordon, 1976) ready for yourself and that other person: 'Ultimate solutions to problems are rational; the process of finding them is not.' It is a legitimate answer and, provided that the end product is effective, valued, liked and efficient, it will be accepted and understood.

4. A thought-up design is ready for working out when you can draw it, explain it clearly to someone else, visualize it with cut-out bits of paper or a bit of string... How you do it is up to you. It's your design.

5. Listen very carefully to what your thought-up design is telling you about introducing the special bit of content that will be the students' REO and focal point of learning. It may want you to introduce it bit by bit or as a whole. It may want you to introduce it straight away in the course or lesson, half-way through, or bit by bit and only at the end in its entirety. In thinking up a design, the REO was of special help to you, the designer. When you have worked out the design (with the REO running through it), the REO must have been woven into the design so that it now works *for your learners* and no longer just for you.

6. Find a desk or a table and a window, or imagine you have these. Put your feet up and reflect on this thought of Albert Einstein: 'The most beautiful thing we can experience is the mysterious. It is the source of all true art and science.'

   Let the pictures that this thought evokes come swimming into the video of your mind.

Chapter 4

Testing and Revising a Design

Introduction

Every freshly made course or lesson is unique. It carries the fingerprint of its designer's design decision-making. The last convolutions in the print come from decisions made as you test-and-revise (activity 4.3) a thought-up, worked-out design. The test is made with the help of a small group of learners, chosen at random but representative of the student population for whom the course or lesson was designed.

In the programme writing practice that I knew in New York in the '60s and '70s, it was the custom to use eight learners in a try-out. Such a 'jury of eight' were able to pick up most of the design mistakes that had been made in preparing self-study programmed learning systems. The eight usually represented a heterogeneous population of several hundred users. Habit, and previous good results, would make me choose eight for testing the design of a new course or lesson today. Practicality might, of course, make one settle for a smaller group of three or four or even two.

Testing for the unexpected

In the developmental testing of a design, you are testing for the unexpected: for unexpected wrong responses, unexpected interfering responses and unexpected attitudes of learner and teacher (if one is involved). These things are 'unexpected' because with the help of the four referents and the protocol for working out a design, you have done your best to avoid unwanted results. But in this respect, 'all that glitters is not gold'. You must expect the unexpected. The symptom that all is not what it should be is an unexpected low rating on one or more of the elements in the *Emax Vmax Lmax E′max* criteria.

Table 6: *A video presentation test result*

Effective	Valued	Liked	Efficient
+	+	+	+
+ +	+ +	− −	+ +
+	+	+	+
±	+	+	+
+	+	∓	+
∓	∓	∓	− −
+	+	+	+
+	+	∓	+
+	+	−	+ +
+	+	−	+

In Table 6 you can see the results from a test of the reaction of ten learners to a video presentation. The film was 20 minutes long and in colour. It aimed to teach the set up of an experiment in physiology on the effect of chemical and electrical stimuli on the heart rate of an anaesthetized frog. Set up of the

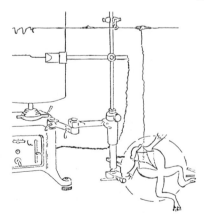

experiment involved anaesthetizing the frog, opening its chest to expose the heart, and the attachment of a measuring device to the exposed heart. The surgical operation is a delicate one. Mistakes are easily made. These can lead to bleeding and the need for intervention by an experienced laboratory teacher. Irreparable damage to the heart can also occur. If the damage is irreparable, the set up must be begun all over again with a second anaesthetized frog. The class for whom the teaching film was made consisted of 70 students. What do you make of the results in the development test group (Table 6)?

One student has quite different views about the teaching quality of the film from the rest. What would you do with such a contradiction? Anything? What do you think is accounting for a consistently low rating on 'liking' the film? Would you think the film is didactically a success?

The questions above are the sort of questions which will challenge your skill as a diagnostician and troubleshooter when you get back the results from a developmental test of a course or lesson or of a single S-R event. You will need your intuition, creativity, and logical thinking to tell you what to do. When things turn out to be *very* unexpected you will need the courage to go back into your think tank and re-think the whole design. When things are relatively good (the majority rating high and a minority rating low) you have to decide how to make any necessary changes at a minimum cost. Sometimes this will take a lot of didactic cunning. The chances are that you will already have invested quite a lot of time and energy in thinking up and working out the design.

Some common mistakes

In the beginning, every designer makes a lot of mistakes. You never stop making them, in fact, but they grow less in number as your experience grows. Most are made in working out the design — in giving the abstract idea its concrete form. In my experience as a mistake maker, there are eight special ones which you have to guard against. They are listed below.

The missing imperatives

Learners can like being told what to do. 'Think aloud', 'Draw a diagram', 'Talk to yourself about . . .', 'Label this picture', 'Explain this to . . .', 'Match the items in List A with those in list B', 'Conjure up a mental picture of . . .', 'Explain to your neighbour . . .', 'Listen to the silence in this film' — these are some of the imperatives you can use to sharpen the pace of the learning process.

'Make the connection between . . . and . . .', 'Paraphrase', 'Solve this', 'Translate', 'Work out', 'Stop and think', 'Give yourself two minutes to . . .', 'Rewrite this', Underline', 'Cross out', 'Fill in', 'Look up', 'Throw out . . .'.

Imperatives demand action and attention. Without them a learning experience can be too passive. Their absence can slow down the tick-tick-tick of an effective, fast-moving, learning process.

The missing overview

Learners like to know where they are going. They need some navigational aid (verbal or visual) at the very start of the course or lesson which maps out, or hints at, the response route they are going to take. In the world of design at the micro level, this is often called an 'overview'. This overview can, in a subtle way, anticipate things which later in the course or lesson will be very critical. Like an overture, an overview creates a mood and a reason for wanting to start and to go on. An overview must convey why it's worthwhile to be attentive and to do what will be asked of you as a learner. Below is one example. It is the overview to the refresher course for young GPs on the subject of dermatology in general practice. This course was the subject of case study no. 3 in Chapter 3. The overview begins with a statement to motivate the learner's interest. The statement is a reflection of an experienced physician on the profile of a 'good doctor'. He formulates this profile for all GP's out of the qualities he would like in a doctor treating a member of his own family.

Introduction

'If I ask a colleague to look after a member of my family, I ask these sorts of questions: Does he care? Does he try? Does he visit patients? Does he get up at night? Does he listen? Does he examine? Does he talk with patients' relatives? Does he *know*?' (John Horder, President, Royal College of General Practitioners, London.)

We hope the exercises and information which you are asked to work through in this book will help you 'know' something more about the recognition, assessment and treatment of skin disorders (dermatoses) in general practice.

In each exercise you are asked to *do* something: answer a question, make a diagnosis, decide a treatment, study a diagram, look something up or process some information. Most times, but not always, you will be given *feedback information*. This information is for use *after* you have done what has been asked of you. It will help you evaluate the 'correctness' of your own response.

Togther the exercises are designed to refresh your knowledge of dermatology and to stimulate more fruitful discussion around patient problems in our group sessions.

Without an overview, learners are too often thinking and listening in their own frame of reference and the teacher is thinking and teaching in her or his. There may be no communication because wrong associations are being made on both sides. The overview is very critical in establishing a common frame of reference. Out of this frame of reference the teaching-learning process can begin with student and teacher understanding its purpose, knowing its end goal and understanding each other.

The impracticality of a design

'Nice', 'good', 'beautiful', 'exciting', but remaining for ever gathering dust in its worked-out form on the designer's shelf: this is sometimes the fate of a good design. The designer involved has not been sensitive enough to the *practicality* of the design. A worked-out design must be capable of installation in the systems for which it was made. This means that at the time of developmental testing there must be care for such things as 'how is the new course or lesson going to be received by teachers as well as by students?', 'what rostering difficulties (if any) are going to come up?', 'will there be time and space problems?', 'does the design demand training of teachers and their assistants?', 'is the design just too new and too different to be accepted in an existing and perhaps conservative curriculum?'. Impracticality can be the Achilles' heel of a good design.

The missing melody

An S-R event in which the primary goal is 'to instruct' has a sharp, business-like sound to it. It has to deliver some predefined knowledge or skill. In contrast, an S-R event which is an 'encounter' gives the learner plenty of room to respond in her or his own way. An encounter has no end-performance goal. It has an evocative sound to it. Events which have to 'explain' or to 'tell' have goals and sounds somewhere in between. In the Think Tank workshop we nickname these four types of event 'ching', 'chang', 'chung' and 'chong' events (see Table 7).

Table 7: *The sounds of an S-R event*

A	B	C	D
to instruct	to instruct	to instruct	to instruct
to explain	*to explain*	to explain	to explain
to tell	to tell	*to tell*	to tell
to let encounter	to let encounter	to let encounter	*to let encounter*

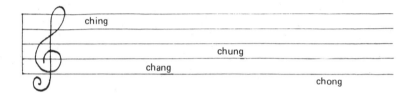

The primary goal in an event decides which type it is. From a didactical point of view, the best S-R event is a melody of 'ching', 'chang', 'chung' and 'chong'. A good lecture, for example, is a 'chung' event with lots of 'chong'. Its primary goal is to *tell* something of importance. But it must also explain, and to some degree instruct. More than anything, if what is told is to be remembered long after the lecture is over, the lecture must be a vivid encounter. The melody of a good lecture is 'chung, chong, chang, ching'. The sound of the primary goal (chung) blends with the sound of an encounter (chong); the sound of explanation (chang) and the sound of a bit of instruction (ching) join them to make an inspiring lecture.

Listening for the missing melody (the missing ching, or the missing chang, etc) can tell you a lot about *less than maximum results* in a developmental test of a design. Hearing the melody and at the same time recognizing its source can tell you about a course's or lesson's bright success.

The non-integration problem

How many times as a teacher or designer have you heard the complaint that the separate parts of a course 'don't seem to belong to each other'? You have probably had to respond to the complaint of non-integration in a course or lesson more than once. It's a common problem. Usually, in my experience, the fault stems from a faulty decision over the learning sequence — over the student's 'response pathway' through the content of the course. Below is an example close to home. It is about the 'non-integration' of concepts and content in an eight-day course on 'course development'. The teachers involved are using the 'course development activities cycle' from this book as their special bit of content, ie their REO. This cycle is the one shown in Fig. 1, repeated here in Fig. 15. The course begins with the subject of activity 1, moves on to activity 2 and so on, in a clockwise direction. Each activity is handled by a different teacher.

The students like the course. They value it enough to recommend it to their fellow students. In principle the melody is there for both the teachers and the students. *But* ... they don't find it very effective, nor do they find it very efficient. They miss the integration of the course's parts.

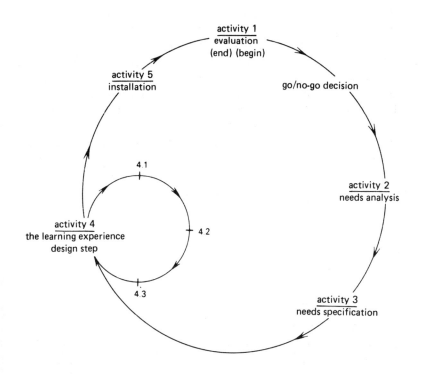

Figure 15 *A course development activities cycle.*

79

The problem is one of *sequence.* The five parts of the course (corresponding to the five activities in the circle) need to be taught in an *anticlockwise sequence.* In this way, the part which is being given has a clear and logical relationship to the parts which have come before. The course in anticlockwise sequence would look like this:

Part 1 End Evaluation: In this part, I learn (as a student) about the good and less good results of a course or lesson. I learn about assessment; about what assessment is and how to do it properly. I exercise my skill . . .

Part 2 Installation: I am now in a good position to look for and understand what things in the installation of a course (the teaching-learning process itself) account for good and less good results in an end evaluation. I know about these because I have already learned about what I will, at the end of my course or lesson, be testing for. I learn about communication and the management of the teaching-learning process . . .

Part 3 Learning Experience Design: Knowledge of evaluation and installation tells me that good things and less good things in a learning experience have a lot to do with its *design*, ie with the plan, structure and strategy of instruction that (depending on its quality) will add music and/or noise to the installation and the end result . . . As a student I can integrate what I have learned and exercised in parts 1 and 2 with what I am learning now about design in part 3 . . .

Parts 1, 2 and 3 provide the logical background and frame of reference for new things in *part 4 (needs specification).* Parts 1, 2, 3 and 4 provide the background and give meaning to things about *needs analysis (part 5).* Eventually I complete my backward journey by returning to the subject of *evaluation*, but this time with an eye and ear open for things in evaluation that indicate a 'Go' or 'No Go' decision, to revise or not revise an existing course. This anticlockwise sequence has given me what (as a student) I needed. I can integrate the separate subjects in the course.

'Backward chaining', as this reversed sequencing is called (Gilbert, 1962, and Mechner, 1967), has been used to teach problem-solving in geometry, learning to avoid faults in playing a piece of music, teaching children to tie a shoelace, learning to hypothesize, learning to set up a complex experiment in physiology, selling shoes in a shop and waiting on table in a country hotel.

The backward chaining technique is a powerful teaching technique and a powerful integrator.

Some minor but critical faults

'*Tekfrak*', '*tooterm*', '*non crit art*', '*non crit info*', '*transition*', '*wow!*' and '*speed up*' were some of the editing codes used in editing self-study texts in Basic Systems Inc, New York, in the '60s. I learned a lot from these codes. Usually written in red pencil or red ink, there was no escaping them. You had to discover for yourself the critical programming fault that each pointed to and, having done that, put it right. Doctors, fire fighters, refrigeration systems engineers, post office supervisors, salesmen, managers, cashiers, dancers, drop-outs and dentists are just some of the target populations who I know benefited from these codes and the corrections that each signalled. Because the codes were there, the learning experiences of our clients were a little more effective, valued, liked and efficient than they would have been without them. I still use these codes today.

Tekfrak warned you to look at the technical content of some information. For some reason it was suspect and possibly wrong; there was a 'fracture' in it.

Tooterm told you that you were likely to confuse the learner with a term that had not been previously defined. It was being used too early in the text. If you didn't explain it, at or before the indicated point, it was going to give your learner trouble.

Non crit art told you that the artwork (some schema or diagram, picture or photo) was little more than decoration. Your student hadn't been asked to process the information in it. The artwork was non-critical in the learning process. The response you were inviting could probably be made without even referring to the artwork.

In Fig. 16 you will find two versions of an item which is intended to teach a rule about 'looking before crossing the street'. The rule is for a traffic situation in which cars, bicycles, buses and so on drive on the *right-hand* side of the street. The example is a simple one but it illustrates 'critical and non-critical use of artwork' in an item that has to teach.

Non crit info tells you that some information you are using in a course or lesson is 'non-critical information'. In its existing form, place or content, it is adding nothing to the learning process. Information is 'critical' only if it is necessary for a

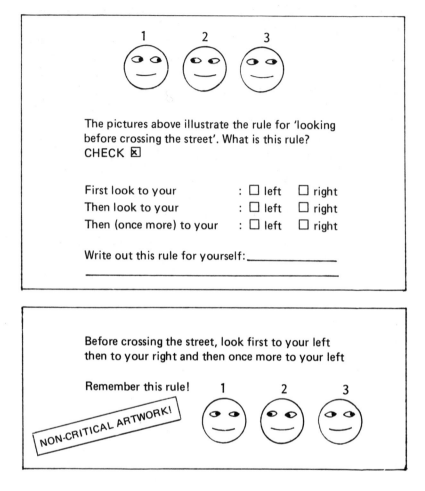

Figure 16 *Critical and non-critical artwork.*

correct response, or prevents a wrong response, or excludes some interfering response, or is important for some affective component in the learning process. The development of a value or a desired attitude are examples of components in the 'affective' area of learning.

Transition indicates an unsmooth or confusing move from one S-R event to another. It can be a timely warning that at this point in your course or lesson you are likely to be losing some learners. You need to tighten or clean up something at this spot. Continuity is important in a worked-out design.

Wow! tells you to beware. You may be using some example or anecdote that would hurt the sensibility of someone in your audience — your learner will express a mental (and sometimes verbal) 'wow!'. This coded item reminds you to be alert to possible sensitive reactions from your learner population. Not all learners share your own prejudices and sense of humour!

Speed up tells you that the pace of learning is too slow. You are being told to speed it up. The secret of doing this, in my experience, is to make better 'music' in some critical S-R events. You need to get the elements of instruction, explaining, telling and letting encounter to serve each other better. This will shorten both your and your learner's tasks.

An always avoidable fault

This refers to any breakdown in the relationship between components in referent 2 (the nth generation of the specified needs).

Not long ago I was working with a new subject for a new exercise in the Think Tank workshop. Participants had to design a course for spies. They had to teach their spy-students how to lip read. Referent 2 was indispensible in deciding who of the

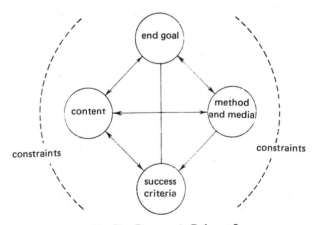

The Five Elements in Referent 2

spy population needed to learn to lip read, how they would be tested, what content (words and language) would be used, what method-and-media (mirrors and fellow spies, for example) would be used and what constraints had to be taken into account. Design decision faults when they related to content and relationships in the workshop participants' referent 2 were quickly traced. When the exercise was over we discussed the quality of the proposed design. In looking critically at their decision-making, participants knew that faults which sat in their databanks (referent 2) need never have been made!

A fault in your specification of the needs (the data in your databank) is always an avoidable fault. Referent 2 'programs' you to make decisions that ensure that the basic ingredients of the design ('end goal', 'success criteria', 'content' and 'method-and-media') complement each other and that the decisions about each respect existing 'constraints'. When you, as a designer, fail to respond to this 'program', you will only have yourself to blame when breakdowns between the components manifest themselves in the form of poor learning results during developmental testing and/or in an end evaluation of your worked-out design.

A fundamental fault

If I were a millionaire, I would give away T-shirts with a special emblem; designers of instruction (myself included) would get four each. The emblem reminds us of a fundamental truth about ourselves and about our students. This truth has been mentioned before (Chapter 1, page 28): each of us has four quadrants in our make-up. If, in thinking up and working out designs, we forget this, we will have made a *fundamental fault*.

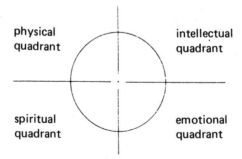

Our most effective and efficient designs will not be valued and will not be liked. Nor will our most valued and liked design be effective and efficient. A design is something we experience. It touches the intellectual, emotional, spiritual and physical in us. A designer of instruction needs to be constantly aware of this in thinking up and working out a design and in interpreting the results obtained in developmental testing of a design.

You have met eight common faults which you may have to diagnose and cure when you test a worked-out design. There are, of course, very many more which could also have stolen into the design despite the use of the four referents and care in working out your design. You will find that a knowledge of faults is not only significant for troubleshooting worked-out designs at the time of developmental testing, but it also helps you think up better designs, work out designs in a better way and be a better diagnostician of things that have gone wrong. In time, you will find yourself thinking up, working out and testing designs *all at the same time* in your think tank. This is a signal that you have the art and craft of the design of instruction coming into your fingertips. You'll see it in the 'fingerprint' that your decision-making will put on your courses or lessons: their designs will be effective, valued, liked and efficient.

Case study no. 5: Riding out the storm

In this case study we return to the Botany students and their encounter with the use of the scientific method of enquiry into the phenomenon of apical dominance in plants. The results, you will remember, were not all that we hoped for in this think-and-do-for-yourself type of experiment. The encounter in most groups scored too low on effectiveness ($\mp$) and efficiency ($\mp$). What was the problem? What was the solution?

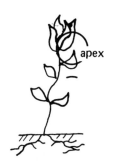

One contributory factor was certainly a fault of my own as the most experienced course designer in the team. I had forgotten a golden rule of course designers: always involve *all* the teachers who are going to teach in the making of their course. Out of nine group leaders (teachers and teaching assistants) we had only been working with five. Four had never been given the chance to make the new-style experiment their own. When the time came to install the course, the new 'plan, structure and strategy of instruction' was for these four a relative stranger. In some respects it was also an unfriendly one!

A second contributory factor was the heterogeneous composition of the student groups. Some students were surprisingly competent and original in their hypothesizing. Others were not. The best found the step-by-step learning process a bit of a nuisance and not efficient. They wanted, in fact, to teach themselves.

Many students meant many plants. Many plants required much space. The teaching-learning situation in the laboratory was not the easiest to manage. This was a third factor which made the learning experience less effective and less efficient than it might have been.

A fourth contributing factor was a group leader difference. Some leaders were not as experienced as, for example, the two teachers who initiated the new-style experiment. A teacher's guide which was designed to minimize this problem was not as helpful as had been hoped.

What was the solution?

This was one of the rare occasions in design decision-making when it made sense to let the worked-out design (with its problems) ride out the storm. From the positive reactions that we had got we knew there was a good chance that some of the problems should correct themselves. We knew that both the teachers and the curriculum would benefit from further experience in working with this type of design. For safety's sake I had a contingency solution in my mind. The back-up solution concentrated on giving more chance for teachers and students to speed up or slow down the learning process. It made use of a spiral sequence (see Chapter 3, page 61). Five S-R events (A to E) were involved, and three levels of learning were possible.

Event A would become an each-time-around teacher intervention. Events B, C, D and E would involve real (or on paper) exercises in, successively, 'phenomenon observation', 'general hypothesis formulation', 'work hypothesis formulation' and 'hypothesis testing plus the drawing of conclusions'. Students could be seen entering the spiral of S-R events singly or in small groups. Their level of entry was determined by their knowledge of the phenomenon of apical dominance and their knowledge and skill in the use of the scientific method of enquiry. In principle they would move at their own pace along an upward, spiralling pathway to the experiment's end goal. Their point of entry was to be determined in consultation with the laboratory teacher in the first intervention event.

Some tips

1. Look at the following diagram. The gymnastics of thinking up, working out and testing designs overlap. Let this fact register itself in some corner of your mind.

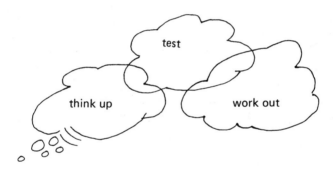

    The diagram will remind you that *because of this overlap*, increasing your skill in any one of the processes will increase your skill in the other two.

2. As a troubleshooter of designs, it's good to remember a line from Simon (1966) on the subject of problem-solving: 'Small hints can have dramatic effects on the ease of solution of a problem.'

3. Find the date of your birthday in your diary. Give yourself an advance present by writing this English translation of an old Oriental thought:

> If you give someone a fish
> He can only feed himself once
> If you teach him how to fish
> He will always be able to feed himself.

It will remind you that, as a designer or designer-teacher or troubleshooter you must always want to teach your students *how to fish!*

4. Next time you eat a tomato, think about the phenomenon of apical dominance in plants. Tomato plants exhibit apical dominance. At the same time think about the steps in the

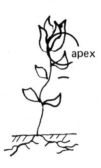

scientific method of enquiry. Disciplined thinking is as much a *sine qua non* for course and lesson design decision-making as it is for effective application of the scientific method.

5. As an idea for a design goes rocking and vibrating its way through your mind, keep your decision-making clean, clear and uncluttered. Stay objective in the excitement of your creativity!

Chapter 5
Installation and End Evaluation

Introduction

It's time to close the circle, and say something about the last two activities in the course design activities cycle: the *installation* of the course or lesson in the learner's programme, and the *end evaluation* of the design. This latter event is the moment of truth. Its result will tell you how successful you have been as a designer in thinking up, working out, testing-and-revising and installing your worked-out design.

Installation

Once a course or lesson has been tested and revised, it is ready for *installation* (activity 5, Fig. 1) in the system to which it belongs. This system could be a curriculum in a distance learning system such as in correspondence or radio or television network learning. It could be the programme of a kindergarten, a lower school or a high school. It could be a self-study modularized curriculum in vocational training. It could be a system of evening classes in butter making, knitting, nuclear physics, painting, first aid, car repair, or public speaking. As the designer or designer-teacher you have to make sure that the system into which your course or lesson is brought is going to help and not

activity 5
installation

hinder the S-R events in which the learner (and teacher if there is going to be one) is going to be involved.

You will usually need to be an arranger, a go-between, a persuader and a constraints beater. You may also need to be a teacher-of-the-teacher, or a setter-up and troubleshooter of electronic hardware. Your task in installing the course or lesson is to ensure that there are no distractions in the system that will interfere with the working of your design.

A good installation will care for a kaleidoscope of things. These can include: good accommodation, carefully scheduled breaks, provision of reference materials for those who would like them, smooth running feedback systems, clear programmes, back-up equipment for use in the event that equipment on location breaks down, coloured chalk, coffee and tea, public transport timetables, places where students and teachers can wash themselves and hang up their coats, facilities for making a telephone call. Being a designer of a course or lesson also requires you to be a manager of the teaching-learning scene when the time comes to install what you have helped create.

On-the-spot designing

Once a course or lesson has been installed and is in progress, the design takes over. Students and teacher (if there is one) and materials and the design rock back and forth and interact with each other in a 'response environment' for learning. If your decision-making has been good in creating this environment there is a good chance that it will have success. Your students will learn and will learn in a way that they like.

But, no designer can foresee and cater for every individual need. There will always be some *on-the-spot-designing* to be done: a left-handed sheep shearer is having difficulties in an exercise that has been written (unwittingly) for only right-handed sheep shearers; an educational visit to the Van Gogh museum in Amsterdam has allowed too little time for questions to which learners would like an answer; three medical students have bought microscopes of low quality — it is handicapping their work in cell biology; a singing teacher turns up at her Music Academy with a sore throat; one student in a class (who really wants to learn) can't keep up with the rest. When a teacher is involved, she or he must take care of such things, and in doing so modify or extend the design. She or he must do some *ad hoc* on-the-spot designing.

The left-handed sheep shearer will probably best be helped by a joke about right-handed designers, and friendly personal instruction. The fans of Van Gogh need to be promised another opportunity for asking their burning questions. The medical students with the low-quality microscopes will need to negotiate with fellow students for the use of a good microscope for some of the critical laboratory tasks. The sore-throated teacher could perhaps substitute herself with a long-playing record . . . But when thinking about how you are going to use your intuition, logical thinking and creativity in doing any necessary on-the-spot designing, don't forget that *prevention* is probably always better than cure. You must learn as a designer or teacher to look ahead and *provide for safety first!*

Designs for courses and lessons in which a teacher is not involved (eg self-study units) can have built-in remedial pathways to take care of on-the-spot design problems. The learner is informed about these pathways and is free to take them on her or his own initiative. Their existence offers the learner a special degree of control over the learning process. In making use of remedial pathways the learner is in fact doing a bit of on-the-spot designing for her or himself.

End evaluation

Once a course or lesson you have designed is over, you will need to look into the mirror of an *end evaluation* (activity 1). You will need to validate the quality of your own design decision-making. This end evaluation is always a moment of truth. You will be surprised (sometimes pleasantly and sometimes not so pleasantly) at what you see. Was the design a didactical success? Was there too much on-the-spot designing

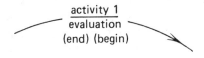

activity 1
evaluation
(end) (begin)

to be done? Was the design easy to work with? How did the students experience the design?

As the designer you are now interested in:

1. the didactical effect of the design
2. the quality of each student's learning experience
3. how the design fitted into the system

There are very few designs which will not need some modification before the course or lessons they steer are given a second time.

Case study no. 6: Troubleshooting refrigeration systems

The usual long, hot summer. In Townville, Illinois, manager Joseph D Doe of the Buy-It-Here supermarket chain is getting hot under the collar. For the sixth time in three days he is listening to another complaint from one of his branch managers about 'poor freezer maintenance service'. There is a pattern in the complaints which come from different areas in the state.

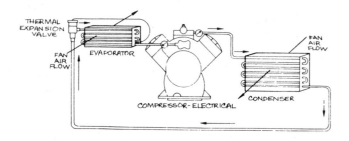

A freezer cabinet or cool room malfunctions. A service engineer arrives, looks, works on the system and gets it going again. Some four hours later the system is again out of operation. Withdrawal of products from freezers and cool rooms in which the temperature has risen above safe limits is beginning to bite into branch profits. Joseph D Doe reaches for the phone...

Incidents like this once prompted a supplier of refrigerants to create a course on the *Systematic troubleshooting of refrigeration systems* (E I du Pont de Nemours, 1964). The course was constructed around an algorithm (decision-making tree) via which each subsystem in a refrigeration unit — the condenser, evaporator, thermal expansion valve and compressor electrical system — was subjected to a systematic troubleshooting regime. Through this procedure the stop-start-stop problems which were known to plague users of refrigeration and air conditioning installations were minimized.

Imagine you are Joseph D Doe. You have chosen to send your 15 service engineers (in groups of five) on a course which makes use of the procedure referred to above. The course lasts two days. It covers both theory and practice. The post-test consists of a performance test in which course participants have to demonstrate their skill in diagnosing and correcting three malfunctions, using the systematic troubleshooting decision tree taught in the course. Critical theoretical knowledge relating to the procedure is tested with the help of written responses to multiple-choice questions, and an oral test given by an instructor not involved in the teaching of this particular course. As

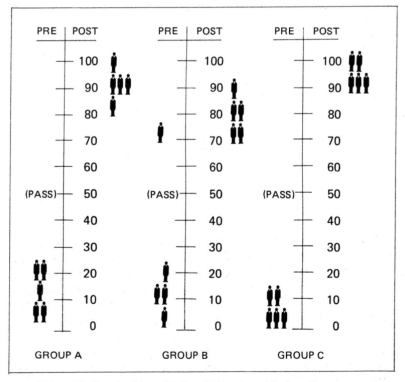

Figure 17 *Results from the Buy-It-Here troubleshooting course.*

Joseph D Doe you want some guarantee of the efficiency of the course. A pre-test of the service engineers' individual knowledge and skill is requested. The results of the pre-test and post-test for the three groups of engineers are given in Fig. 17.

What do you think of these results? Would you be satisfied with them? Under what conditions would you trust the validity of both tests? Would you recommend this course to other supermarket chains on the basis of the engineer's end results? Engineers scoring 50 points or more on the combined practice-and-theory tests will have satisfied the course makers' criterion for a participant's success.

Case study no. 6 generates a lot of questions as well as a lot of answers when it is given in the Think Tank workshop. Discussions, questions and answers tend to run along the following lines.

As Joseph D Doe, most Think Tank workshop participants are satisfied — at first glance — with the end results. One hundred per cent of the Buy-It-Here engineers have scored 70 points or more on the final test: 20% the perfect score, 46% 90 points and 34% 70 points. With one exception (an engineer in group B) there is no indication in the results of the pre-test that existing knowledge of and skill in the systematic trouble-shooting procedure which the course set out to teach was contributing to these end results.

A condition for trusting the validity of the apparent high success is that both pre- and post-test were so comprehensive that *everything the course intended to teach was tested for.* Joseph D Doe would need assurance of this from some test specialist (with appropriate technical knowledge of the trouble-shooting system being taught) from outside the course.

Twenty per cent of the Buy-It-Here service engineers have a perfect score. What should one think about that? One should be suspicious of such results until there is the assurance (as hinted at above) that the test is comprehensive and therefore valid. But one should not be surprised once the result is known to be a valid one. Short, practical courses which have been develop-mentally tested (with the help of the jury of eight, for example) before installation should be expected to deliver top end performance results. Joseph D Doe should have no hesitation in recommending the course when the appropriate test conditions exist.

What Joseph D Doe should be interested in is the apparent difference in performance between group B and groups A and C.

The service engineer with the high pre-test score would certainly be worth talking to. What sort of things might account for this group difference? 'Installation problems' and 'motivation problems' are both brought up as possible causes in our discussions on this point in the Think Tank workshop. Such might well be the problem. Motivation and lack of motivation (possibly on the part of the engineer with the high pre-test score) are both infectious! Especially so in a course with a sharp end performance goal.

The long, hot summer continues. Joseph D Doe relaxes. From time to time he talks with his chief service engineer about the results of the troubleshooting course. As he listens to the most recent report, a contented smile comes over his face. At that moment the telephone rings. A complaining voice crackles in his left ear...

Everything that shines can't always shine like gold. Even after an effective and efficient training programme you still have to keep an eye on things!

[By the way, what had the designer of the troubleshooting course used as the REO — the system of stimuli which generated the responses needed for learning? If you have some knowledge of condensers, evaporators, thermal expansion valves and compressor electrical things, what do you think the designer put in the databank (referent 2) when thinking up the plan, structure and strategy of instruction for this course? If you have some technical knowledge, try to fill a referent 2 for yourself.]

In case study no. 6 a performance test, multiple-choice questions and oral questions were mentioned as being used to test the knowledge and skill of the 15 engineers. Essay tests, short answer tests, anecdotal records, rating scales, true—false items and matching items are also used to test what an individual has learned or not learned as a result of the design that has been used. So too are such activities as presentations, problem-solving, carrying out an experiment successfully, writing a poem, making a video product — any activity, in fact, which is appropriate for indicating the individual student's achievement of the intended learning goal.

In practice, it is not usually possible to make use of a *pre-test*. You generally have to work only with the results of a post-test, especially when the number of students is large and it is the teacher who has to prepare, administer and grade the pre- and post-test results. Instead, you must rely upon the accuracy of your 'Go' decision, needs analysis and needs specification. You must work on the assumption that the students 'entering profile' is not contributing significance to the end result. If it does, they don't need to be on the course.

In addition to knowing the *didactical effect* of your design, you also need to know how each student *experienced* the design.

'Experiencing' a design

A physics teacher is using vivid analogies in her lesson on the subject of 'sound and silence'. The analogies are understood by all except two of her students. The two are wanting and willing to learn. Both fail a test at the end of the lesson.

A paper dart wings its way across a sixth-form classroom during a lesson on computer programming. The student aircraft manufacturer has nothing better to do. His knowledge and skill in computer programming puts him far ahead in the class.

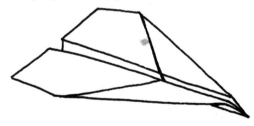

Sergeant M of the Chicago Police Department is having difficulties in keeping awake. He is an unwilling participant in a course on 'rules of evidence' given by a lawyer.

Three children on an educational visit to a picture gallery are so tired they can't listen to their guide anymore....

I like to explore the quality of the individual learner's experience of a design with the help of four critical questions. The questions can be asked personally (when there are not too many students involved) or asked via a written questionnaire. The questionnaire with the four questions is given in Table 8.

Table 8: *Four critical questions*

Questionnaire

1. Was there something you felt you needed in this learning experience and didn't get?

---

2. Would you recommend this course/lesson to someone else? (To whom? Why? Why not?)

---

3. What is your *sharpest* memory of this learning experience?

---

4. How would you rate your learning experience as a whole in terms of its effectiveness, value to you, enjoyability and efficiency?

Here are some reactions which I have met via the questionnaire in Table 8:

> 'I felt a lack of personal contact between me and the teacher.'
> 'The problems we were given were not sophisticated enough.'
> 'Too much listening and not enough doing'.
> 'I don't want to be required to do an experiment on a frog. I need an alternative choice of experiment.'
> 'We never covered this.'
> 'We needed to hear theories that disagreed with the theory in this course.'
> 'More coffee breaks.'.

Question 1 usually brings a kaleidoscope of needs to light. Most can be related to one or more of the quadrants in the respondent's make-up.

Recommendations and non-recommendations and no recommendations (question 2) can put a finger on the strong and weak aspects of your beautiful design! An introductory evening course on music theory is recommended for doctors because through it they can learn to listen. A course for managers on computer programming turns out to be too technical: the majority of manager participants recommend it for their assistants but not for manager colleagues.

Bad memories and good memories are the ones that persist when a course or lesson is over. Both come up in answers to question 3 in the questionnaire:

> 'I felt I was on a train which stopped at every station. I disliked the 'programmed' strategy which was used.'
> 'My sharpest memory is of the third reading assignment: John Stewart Collis' unforgettable book, *Vision of Glory*.'
> 'I kept thinking: I wish I had had this course three years ago....'

97

Question 4 makes use of our old friends the *Emax Vmax Lmax E'max* criteria. It's always valuable to talk personally to students whose rating on one or more of the items turns out to be very different from that of the rest of the students. As a designer you will want to know what accounts for the difference and to find out what you can do to help the one involved.

Try out the four critical questions on yourself. Think back to yesterday, last week, last month, last year, and to the last course or lesson you were in. Did you like it? Would you recommend it? What (if anything) was wrong with it? Would you find it worthwhile to change its design? Talk to yourself with the questionnaire in mind.

With the help of information about the didactical effect and quality of the experiencing of your design, you are very nearly home. You have one more thing to do: talk to the teacher (who may be yourself) about the quality of the design. Ask questions. 'Was the design difficult to install?', 'Was there much on-the-spot designing to be done?', 'Was it all worthwhile?', 'How would you like to teach this course or lesson again?'. Listen to the answers.

There will usually be some re-designing to be done. You will usually have to speed once more around the circle (see Fig. 1, page 14). You will be cleaning up some design decision-making made in round one. But you will be moving very fast. Your end goal and success this second time around is never very far away.

'Ching-chang-chung-chong
chong-chung-chang-ching...'

It may help to hum a tune along the way.

Review and Exercises

Levels of design decision-making

Didactical design decision-making takes place at three levels. Policy decisions are made at the macro level. Curriculum plans and statements are made at the meso level. The courses and lessons implied in the curriculum statements are created at the micro level. At the micro level the designer is faced with the very specific question: 'What design (didactical strategy) can I use in this piece of instruction for these students so that they will learn what they need to learn in a meaningful way, and in a way that each of them values?'

Design

A design is something we experience. It exists first as a concept in the privacy of the designer's mind. It must then be given concrete form (be worked out). In the case of a course or lesson, the design is the plan, structure and strategy of instruction, conceived so as to produce learning experiences that lead to pre-specified learning goals. A shoe, a chair, a spaghetti fork, a piece of research, a course and a lesson all have a design.

Stimulus-response (S-R) language

The S-R paradigm is the recommended language for use in a dialogue with oneself or others while thinking up, working out and testing-and-revising a design at the course or lesson level. The S-R paradigm sees the events in a course or lesson as stimulus-response events. The event must contain the appropriate stimuli (S) to which the learner responds (R) and, as a result of this response (R), learns. The S-R paradigm contains, in principle, the prescription for any learning event.

Learning experience

A learning experience (Tyler, 1949) refers to 'the interaction between the learner and the external conditions in the environment to which he can react'. Well designed learning experiences will respect (and take explicitly into account) the truth that a person is made up of an intellectual, emotional, spiritual and physical quadrant.

Design success

An indicator of a design's success is the learner's rating of the learning experience (which the design generates) as effective, valued, liked and efficient. The goal of every designer of a course or lesson or teaching-learning event is that it will score high against the $Emax$ $Vmax$ $Lmax$ $E'max$ criteria; E = effective, V = valued, L = liked and E' = efficient. A design which is efficient is a design in which the learning goal is met with a minimum expenditure of time and energy.

Design decision-making process

The course or lesson design process usually begins with an evaluation of an existing design. The evaluation data are the basis for a 'Go' or 'No Go' decision. A 'Go' decision is made when the problem and its solution is seen as a plan-structure-and-strategy-of-instruction one. A *needs analysis* leads to a specification of the needs in terms of five things: the end goal, the criteria used to measure end success, the content to be covered en route to the end goal, first thoughts about method-and-media, and the constraints which need to be respected but outwitted. The *needs specification* is the basis for decision-making at the learning experience design step. Learning experience design recognizes three sub-steps: thinking up a design, working out a design, and testing-and-revising a thought-up, worked-out design. Testing and revision of the design is followed by the installation of the course or lesson and an end evaluation. If the end evaluation exposes the need for further work on the design, this is carried out before the course or lesson begins its life (as a regularly offered course or lesson) in its curriculum.

Four referents

Four decision-making aids that can be used to accelerate the process and optimize the choice of a plan, structure and strategy of instruction are: referent 1 (a set of criteria for a good design), referent 2 (the *n*th generation of the specified needs), referent 3 (an appropriate model), and referent 4 (an effective response-environment organizer). Together they make a 'paradigm' which remains in the background providing a framework in which the process of thinking up a design is embedded.

Referent 1

Referent 1 is a set of criteria against which to test an idea that is being thought about as a plan, structure and strategy of instruction. The criteria explicitly stimulate the designer's thinking. They are concerned with:

1. active rather than passive learning
2. the generation of didactically meaningful responses
3. the assignment of control over the learning process to the learner and/or teacher
4. respect for constraints
5. the provision of feedback
6. the critical use of media
7. the possibility of extension to accommodate the needs of slow and/or fast learners
8. the basing of design decisions on the specified needs.

Didactically meaningful responses

The things which the design requires the learner to do must be meaningful. Each must be relevant for the objective, necessary, possible and effective. 'Effective' means that the response (which may be invited or spontaneous) must result in *some increment* in learning or in the *strengthening* of some learning that has already taken place. Many faults in designs are the result of non-meaningful responses.

Assignment of control

A design assigns control of the learning process to the teacher or to the learner or divides it between the two. The teacher may be personally present or merely present in the materials which are being used. The best designs let teachers and learners *share* control of the teaching-learning process. .

Referent 2

Referent 2 is the nth generation of the specified needs. The content of referent 2 is the designer's *current* specification of the end goal, success criteria, content, method-and-media and constraints. The elements in referent 2 change subtly from moment to moment as the design is thought up. Referent 2 acts as the designer's databank and is constantly being corrected and updated as the ideas for a design ebb and flow and vibrate in the designer's mind. The items in the current (nth) specification must always complement each other. Each must also always reflect respect for constraints.

Referent 3

Referent 3 is an existing design which serves as a model and can accelerate the designer's thinking. The existence of the other three referents ensures that the model chosen is an appropriate one. Complete design transplants are strongly discouraged. Transplants kill creativity and original thinking.

Referent 4

Referent 4 is a response environment organizer (REO). REOs are 'special bits of content' which accelerate design decision-making and frequently result in a mental 'click'. The special bit of content triggers a picture in the designer's mind of what the teaching-learning situation is going to be. After migrating into the heart of the design, the same special bit of content serves as an anchor and organizer for the learner. REOs are very personal things. A bit of content serving one designer as referent 4 is not necessarily effective for another designer of a course on the same subject for the same students and with the same goals in mind.

An REO is discovered or invented or meticulously constructed. To qualify as an effective referent 4 a special bit of content must pass a test which reveals its capacity to:

☐ generate the responses needed for learning
☐ serve as the focal point of learning
☐ act as an anchoring idea or organizer
☐ generate an insightful view of the teaching-learning process

It must be chosen with the other three referents in mind.

Types of stimulus-response (S-R) events

In working out a design it is useful to recognize four types of event: those which have to *instruct*, to *explain*, to *tell* and to *let encounter*. The S-R events in the best courses and lessons have elements of instruction, explaining, telling and letting encounter in them. In this book these are nicknamed respectively 'ching', 'chang', 'chung' and 'chong' events.

Sequence

It is useful to recognize five types of sequence when arranging the S-R events in a course or lesson: *chain, necklace, spiral, network* and *hybrid*. A 'backward chain' sequence is one in which the last step in a process or procedure is taught first, the step preceding the last step is taught second, and so on until the first step is reached. A 'spiral squence' allows a subject or topic or skill or attitude to be treated several times and at a successively higher level of complexity. There is never any one best sequence.

Common faults

These include the missing imperatives, the missing overview, impracticality, the missing melody, non-integration, and minor but critical faults such as: technical faults in content, too early use of a term, non-critical use of artwork, use of non-critical information, unclear transitions, insensitivity, and lack of pace. Additional faults include faults in the build-up of the databank and insensitivity to the four quadrants.

On-the-spot designing

Ad hoc designing is done by the teacher (or via a system of alternative 'learning pathways' when no teacher is used) to accommodate unanticipated needs of learners. In this context, prevention is always better than an on-the-spot cure.

End evaluation

In the end evaluation the designer's interest is in the didactical effect of the design, the quality of each student's learning experience, and how the design fits into the system. The quality of the learning experience can be assessed with the help of four questions, which concern: anything the learner might have needed and missed, whether or not the learner would recommend the course or lesson to another student, the sharpest memory of the learning experience, and the student's rating of her or his experience against the *Emax Vmax Lmax E'max* criteria.

Some 'think' exercises

The following exercises invite you to do some design *thinking* and not design decision-making. The latter can only be done when you are in full possession of or have immediate access to *all* the facts that you would need when doing a first evaluation, making a Go or No Go decision, doing a needs analysis and so on, right up to the stage when your decision-making has created a course or lesson that is ready for developmental testing. To emphasize the fact that the exercises are design *thinking* exercises they are named think 1, think 2, think, 3 and think 4. You can do these 'thinks' on your own but you may find it helps to join another reader, or several other readers, and then 'think' together. It is recommended that you think quickly. Give yourself a maximum of 20 minutes for each think.

Think 1

What ideas (for subject matter, goals, plan-structure-and-strategy-of-instruction, and so on) come into your mind when you think about creating a six-hour course on the subject of 'prevention of fire in hotels'? The course is for hotel managers, telephonists, receptionists, kitchen staff, restaurant staff, room staff and maintenance staff. You will need to be thinking about such things as 'learning not to panic', 'being familiar with escape routes and fire fighting systems and how to use them', 'the most common causes of hotel fires', 'how to help guests in an emergency situation', 'combustion theory', etc. Picture the course in progress and the trainees' activities in the video of your mind. How many S-R events do you visualize? How are they sequenced? What is going on in each event? Give each of them a name. Use a name that excites the interest of the trainee and hints at what the event's goal and activities are going to be. What method-and-media are you thinking of using? Why these media? Can you think of a special bit of content (perhaps an incident, or a definition, or a fire prevention rule) that contains the quintessence of the training message that you have in mind? What will your end test (success criterion) be? Will it be the same for each sub-group of the target group?

Think 2

You are a course and lesson designer in a service department of a university. A professor in logic and philosophy has asked you to help him design a 50-minute lesson on the subject of 'fallacious argument'. The class is for first-year students from all university disciplines. It is a required course. The lesson is the first in a series of lessons that have the goal of mobilizing a student's love for logical thinking. The professor is anxious that *all* the 40 students who attend this first introductory class should rate their learning experience as effective, valued, liked and efficient. He wants them to want more! In the class time available he wants the students to have met and to be able to recognize the following fallacies in logic: *argumentum ad verecundiam* (appeal to authority), *argumentum ad misericordiam* (appeal to pity), *argumentum ad ignorantiam* (argument from ignorance), *argumentum ad hominem* (argument to the man) and *tu quoque* (you too). (See definitions and examples in Table A.)

Look into your mind. What do you see? What are the students doing? What is the professor doing? Is use being made of a visitor? of incidents from real life? Are there newspapers around? Are stills from a video film dancing their way into the room? What stimuli are being used? What responses are the professor and his expert knowledge trying to evoke? Think about each of the criteria for a good design — active participation of the learner, meaningful responding, critical use of media, and so on — are they cared for? The professor is giving

Table A: *Examples of fallacious argument*

---

argumentum ad verecundiam (appeal to authority)
A conclusion is based on an appeal to expertise or authority which is not relevant to the conclusion, eg 'The Rietveld garden spade is *the* best: it's used by 90% of professors in the University of Utrecht'.

argumentum ad misericordiam (appeal to pity)
The fallacy occurs any time pity or sympathy is appealed to for the sake of a favourable conclusion, eg 'He was in an orphanage for twelve years! I vote he gets the loan'.

argumentum ad ignorantiam (argument from ignorance)
The fallacy occurs when the truth of something is concluded because it has not been proved not to be true eg 'It has never been proved that there is no Supreme Being, therefore a Supreme Being does exist'.

Argumentum ad hominem (argument to the man)
The fallacy is present when an attack on the person is used in place of a rational argument to disprove an assertion that the person in question has made, eg 'Her conclusions about nuclear armament are questionable. She is a member of women's lib!'.

the *tu quoque* (you too) fallacy
The fallacy exists when one answers a charge by a similar counter-charge, eg your neighbour defends his rudeness to you by pointing out that you are rude to the owner of the local shop.

---

an end quiz so that the students know for themselves whether they have learned (in the relatively short space of 50 minutes) to recognize and distinguish between five types of fallacious argument. What form does the quiz take? Is it written? Verbal? Is it done with the help of a video? What is its content?

When you have finished your think along these lines, visualize your concept for the lesson's plan, structure and strategy of instruction on a blackboard or a sheet of paper. Explain your ideas with the help of this visualization to someone who is interested in new ways of teaching old subjects.

Think 3

Think about the design for a course in which you have to teach the participants the basic facts and drills for escaping from a car that has dived into the water. The mini course must be no longer than 90 minutes long. It is a prerequisite for entering a practical course in which the participants actually do learn to escape (with other passengers) from a car under water. There are 15 learners each time the course is offered. What basic questions are you going to need answered before you can decide on the content of this prerequisite course? Make a list of eight questions. How are you going to involve the learners in a not too theoretical way? Will you use slides? critical pictures? How are you going to get the 'ching, chang, chung, chong' melody into the mini course? Are you going to have time to deal with fear in your course? If so, how? Imagine *yourself* trapped in a car under water: how do you feel? What does this projection say to you about finding a good design? Are safety belts a help or a hindrance in such a situation? How long (in minutes) do you think you would have to escape? Are there some simple rules which you might concentrate on and teach? Pick up the phone (or ask your 'think' partner to pick up the phone) and do a quick needs analysis via someone who you think may be able to tell you what you need to know. Who might that 'someone' be? your neighbour? your bank manager? a local fire chief? Finally, think up an appealing and assuring name for your course.

Think 4

'A customer bursts into tears.'
'An assistant loses her cool.'

. . . .

Think up six events (routine and unusual) from a day at the counter of the 'client service department' of a busy department store. Let the content of the six trigger some ideas for the content and goals of a course on 'client service'. Feel out their combined content as the system of stimuli that could serve as an REO and referent 4 for your course design decision-making. Listen to what the events are saying to you as the designer of the course.

Finally, talk to yourself for a few minutes about being a designer of courses and lessons at the micro level of design decision-making.

What does a designer of instruction do?
What is a design?
Where does the design process at the micro level begin and end?
Is there a special language of design?
What is a learning experience?
How does a designer know when she or he has had success?

107

Bibliography

(1949) Tyler, Ralph W *Basic Principles of Curriculum and Instruction* The University of Chicago Press, Chicago and London.

(1961) Kendler, Howard H A V *Communication Review* Vol. 9, no. 5, Supplement 4, 'Learning theory and A.V. Utilization' ed. Wesley C Meierhenry.

(1962) Gilbert, T F 'Mathetics: the technology of education' New York: *Journal of Mathetics* 1, January.

(1966) Bruner, Jerome S *Toward a Theory of Instruction* Harvard University Press.

(1964) Kerlinger, Fred N *Foundations of Behavioral Research* Holt, Reinhart and Winston Inc, New York.

(1964) Earl, T, et al *Ten Standard Fire Fighting Orders* (Test Copy). Basic Systems Inc., New York and the Forestry Service, USDA (Under Contract No. 13-96, 1964).

(1964) 'Freon' Products Division, E I du Pont de Nemours & Company (Inc) *Systematic Trouble Shooting for Air Conditioning and Refrigeration Systems* E I du Pont de Nemours & Co (Inc), Delaware, New Jersey, USA.

(1966) Simon, Herbert A *The Shape of Automation for Men and Management*, p78; Harper Torchbooks, The Academy Library, Harper & Row, Publishers, New York.

(1967) Mechner, F. 'Behavioral analysis and instructional sequencing' In: *Programmed Instruction. 65th Year Book of the National Society for Programmed Instruction* (part II) Chicago: University of Chicago Press.

(1969) Ausubel, D P, and Robinson, Floyd G *School Learning: An Introduction to Educational Psychology* Holt, Reinhart and Winston Inc, New York.

(1970) Norman, Frank W 'Nosebleed: handling the problem in your office' *Patient Care* (January 30).

(1973) Milligan, S *Small Dreams of a Scorpion* Penguin Books Ltd, Harmondsworth, Middlesex, England.

(1973) Earl, F A *The Four Referents* (Mededeling) Afdeling Onderzoek en Ontwikkeling van Onderwijs, Rijks Universiteitte, Utrecht, Netherlands.

(1974) Stein, Morris I *Stimulating Creativity* Vol. II, 'Individual procedures' Academic Press Inc, New York.

(1976) Gordon, William J J *Synthetics: The Development of Creative Capacity* Collier Books.

(1979) Merck, E *Read the Skin* Frankfurter Strasse 250, 6000 Darmstadt, F R Germany.

(1980) Earl, F A, Everwijn, S E M, and de Melker, R 'Assisting the observation skills of medical students visiting general practices and patients in their homes' In: *Medical Education*, 1980, **14.**

(1981) Kübler-Ross, E *Santa Barbara Lecture* Cassette: Stichting Dr Elisabeth Kübler-Ross/Shanti Nilaya Nederland.

(1983) Earl, T and Luttik, A *Self Study Unit: Dermatology in General Practice* (Internal Publication) Afdeling Onderzoek en Ontwikkeling van Onderwijs/Instituut voor Huisartsgeneeskunde, Rijksuniversiteitte, Utrecht, Netherlands.

(1984) Tennyson, Robert D, and Breuer, Klaus 'Cognitive based guidelines for using video and computer technology on course development' In: *Video in Higher Education*, ed. Ortrun Zuber-Skerritt, Kogan Page, London.